NEW TO GATHER 'ROUND?

Welcome to *Renaissance and Revival*! If you are new to Gather 'Round Homeschool, I want to take a few moments to explain the philosophy, the backstory, and the *how* behind this curriculum and approach.

WHO AM I?

My name is Rebecca Spooner. I have no special accreditation, and I have no certificates of qualification lining my walls. I am just a homeschool parent like you. I am a second-generation homeschooler who is following my mother's footsteps. I have lived and breathed homeschooling for as long as I can remember. As soon as my kids were (probably not quite) old enough, I had a schedule and a plan and a full curriculum prepared for them. I jumped in with both feet, and I floundered and sputtered and made countless mistakes. Homeschooling my kids was harder than I had ever imagined: there were so many kids and so many curriculum options to choose from. Slowly but surely, my vision of my kids gathered around me like a flock of little chicks faded into the realm of naive and impossible. I began a blog and reviewed curriculum and bounced from one thing to the next (sorry, kids). Eventually, my little blog grew and I began traveling, speaking, and writing books, and I even wrote my first Bible curriculum: *More Than Words*. My dream was to continue with the direction I was in—review curriculum, blog, and write. But all that changed in early 2019.

It started with a healthy dose of discontent. Why on earth was I settling? I was choosing curriculum that was suiting my kids but killing me with all the projects and activities and one-on-one (as I bounced from child to child like a Ping-Pong ball), or I was choosing curriculum that was suiting me and compromising a love of learning to keep my sanity. No one was winning; this couldn't be it. One random weekend, as I was praying and asking God, "What now? What now for my business? What now for our homeschool?" I felt like the question was bounced back at me: "What if you could teach all your kids together?" I believe that when Jesus said He came to bring life and life abundantly, He was thinking about our homeschools and families too. He came to bring life and joy and wonder and curiosity and love of learning—if we learn anything from scripture, it is that God is unpredictable and wild and adventurous and exciting. He cares about our homes, and He cares about our relationships with one another. With that one question and with my pencil poised, the entire vision for Gather 'Round Homeschool was born.

ONE UNIT THAT TIES IN ALL YOUR SUBJECTS FOR ALL YOUR KIDS, TAILORED, CUSTOMIZED, EASY, A LAUNCHPAD FOR ADVENTURE AND LEARNING, KINDLING FOR THE FIRE, AND ABOVE ALL ELSE: ALL ABOUT HIM AND ALL FOR HIM.

Within one month, we were taking preorders for something I was still working out in my head. Now we release new units throughout the year so you and your families can explore a different unit every single month.

We also have mini units, a team of writers and designers and illustrators and proofreaders, and an entire community of over 30,000 families standing with us. This is not just a mom making this—this is an entire community creating a curriculum that is working for a vast variety of homeschoolers with a huge scope of styles and needs. And you have just taken the first step in seeing what taking the pressure off and letting love of learning back into your homeschool can do!

WHAT IS THE GATHER 'ROUND DIFFERENCE?

I have personally tried and used or looked at nearly every curriculum on the market, and I can tell you there is nothing like this to even compare to. The closest model or style that comes close to explaining Gather 'Round is a unit study. We take one topic and we tie all subjects into that topic. We cover nine or more subjects in every unit. Even a single page can cross over into two-to-three subjects: science, geography, history, social studies, spelling, writing, Bible, art, grammar, and more! However, unlike any other unit study out there, instead of merely adapting for older or younger students, we created six student notebooks to go with each teacher's guide. These student notebooks span the ages from preschool all the way up to high school and blend in targeted, leveled, and age-appropriate lessons and projects that meet individual needs. We do not put ages on the notebooks to give you discretion to place your child where you feel they fit best. The levels and their recommended age ranges are as follows:

- **PRE-READER:** 3–5 years old (any student not yet reading)
- **EARLY READER:** 6–8 years old
- **EARLY ELEMENTARY:** 8–10 years old
- **UPPER ELEMENTARY:** 10–12 years old
- **MIDDLE SCHOOL:** 12–15 years old
- **HIGH SCHOOL:** 16–18 years old

We bring in Charlotte Mason elements: a feast of education, narration, art, summation and memory work, and—best of all—no busywork! We also heavily bring in unschooling principles with child-directed learning based on themes or topics that interest them and tie in connections. But for moms with lots of kiddos, we also bring in a core principle to make the one-room schoolhouse flow more smoothly and help your kids work more independently, and I call this the Gather 'Round difference. Let's see it in action with a typical day!

A DAY WITH GATHER 'ROUND HOMESCHOOL

READ FROM THE TEACHER'S GUIDE (10–20 minutes)
Call all your children, young and old, to gather around and listen to today's lesson. The lessons are engaging and full of bright pictures and activity breaks to help hold interest. If you'd like, you can have your students color their picture or take notes on their notebooking page while they listen. The more rabbit trails and discussions you have, the longer this time can take. But remember, you're snuggled on the couch in your pj's, sipping tea or coffee, so everyone is relaxed and chill.

HAVE YOUR STUDENTS WORK IN THEIR STUDENT NOTEBOOKS (30–60 minutes)
Once you have read from the Teacher's Guide, each student will pull open his or her student notebook and work on the lessons. Each notebook has about five pages per day.

SO HOW LONG DOES IT TAKE?

How long this takes depends on you and your kids. If time is short, you can easily finish all your subjects in 1 ½–2 hours. Just add math, and you're finished! If you have the time, you can use this as a jumping point to go deeper, research, go on field trips and adventures, and to find videos and have rich discussions, choosing to do this all day! We have included videos and interactive activities on our resources page (scan the QR code on the bottom of this page or find it right on the menu on our website). You can use these to help fill in the lessons, along with the fun hands-on activities for each lesson.

SUPPLIES

Supplies include an atlas or globe, a pencil, colored pencils, watercolors or paint (optional), a Bible, resources for research (books, internet, etc.), and blank pieces of paper for older students (or a computer for paragraphs, articles, and essays). Middle and high schoolers will need a separate journal for their prayer journal or written summaries as well. And that's it!

IS THIS ENOUGH?

Obviously, I believe in this, or I wouldn't be creating it and selling it. But ultimately, you have to decide that for yourself based on your goals and expectations. It takes trust. Trust that love of learning will accomplish more than force-feeding information. Trust that the connections in these units will mean more to your kids than individual subjects carefully separated into the little cubicles of their minds. Rest in the fact that the less pressure you have and the more time you have, the more you can jump into whatever strikes your fancy and do those things you've always wanted to but never had time for. This is your moment. Lay down the comparison for one month, and let's just bring it back to the family couch. Gather 'Round, kids—this month is going to change everything.

May God bless your homeschool this month. May the Creator of creativity inspire you and give you fresh vision, motivation, and excitement in your home. May this month bring you closer together as a family and spark deep conversations that stick. And may God use what is truly His to draw you and your kids even closer to Him.

Love,

Rebecca Spooner

FACEBOOK PAGE: www.facebook.com/gatherroundhomeschool
FACEBOOK GROUP: www.facebook.com/groups/gatherroundhomeschool
INSTAGRAM: www.instagram.com/gatherroundhomeschool
DOWNLOAD OUR APP: app.gatherroundhomeschool.com

RESOURCES

Renaissance and Revival

INTERACTIVE NOTEBOOKING
Follow the prompts in the Teacher's Guide to pause in the middle of the lesson and complete your notebooking page as you go!

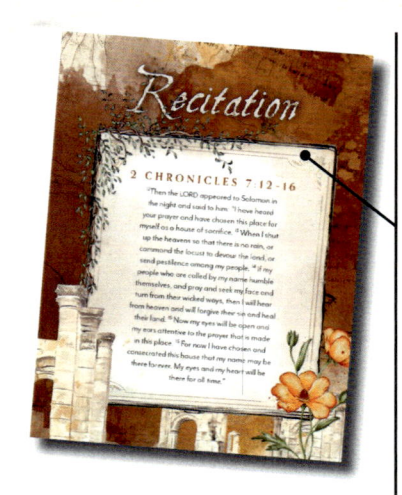

SEATWORK
Try the seatwork
- copywork
- spelling
- vocabulary
- grammar: parts of speech (nouns, pronouns, adjectives, verbs, and adverbs)

RECITATION
In this unit, you will learn about many powerful revivals throughout history. In 2 Chronicles 7:12–16, God promises that if His people humbly pray and seek Him, He will hear, forgive, and bring revival.

WRITING PROJECT
Learn how to read and understand some tricky Shakespearean language, and then plan, write, cast, and perform your very own play!

WE WANT TO HEAR FROM YOU!

Email us and let us know what you think about some of these new features!

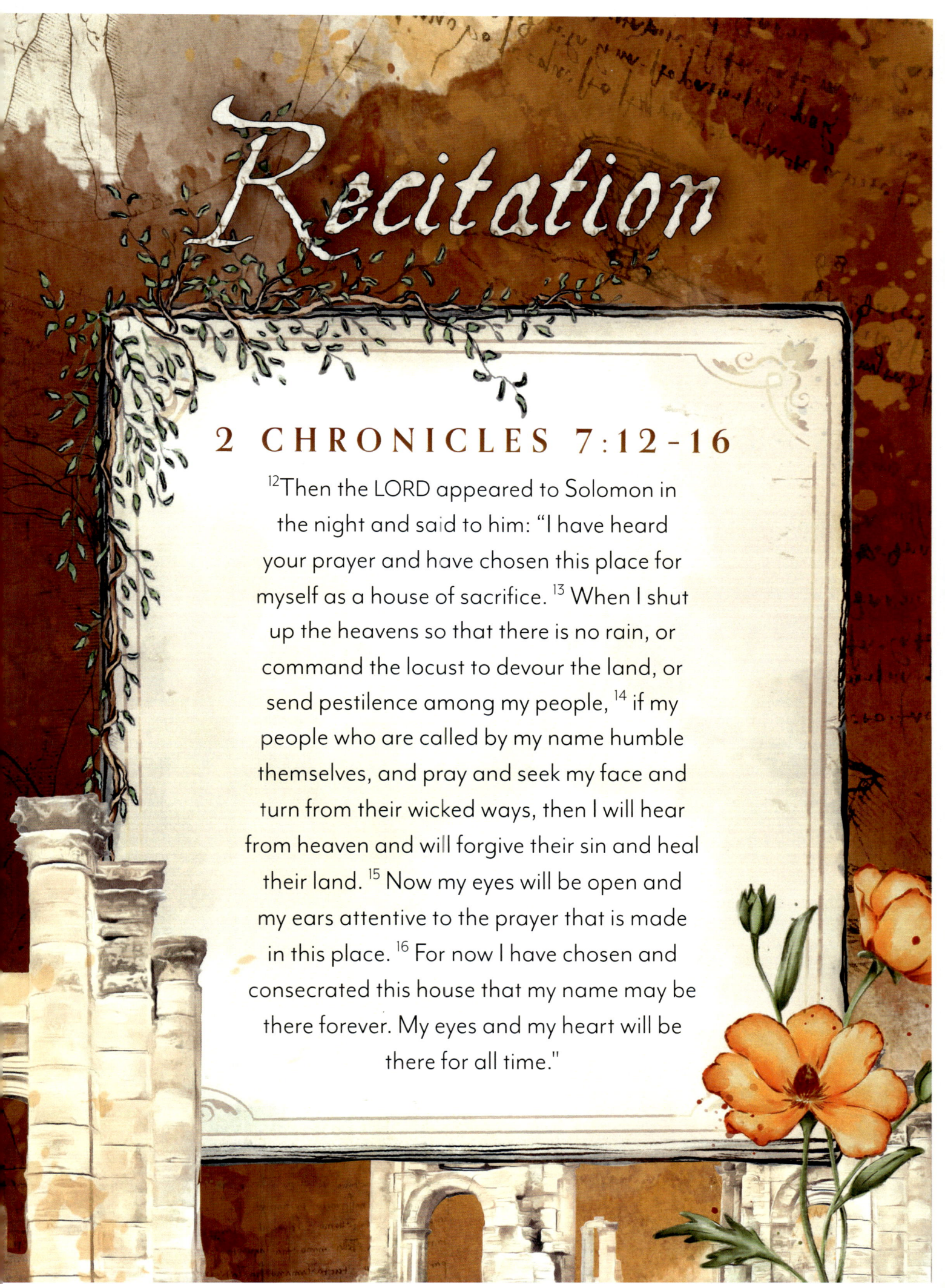

Recitation

2 CHRONICLES 7:12-16

¹²Then the LORD appeared to Solomon in the night and said to him: "I have heard your prayer and have chosen this place for myself as a house of sacrifice. ¹³ When I shut up the heavens so that there is no rain, or command the locust to devour the land, or send pestilence among my people, ¹⁴ if my people who are called by my name humble themselves, and pray and seek my face and turn from their wicked ways, then I will hear from heaven and will forgive their sin and heal their land. ¹⁵ Now my eyes will be open and my ears attentive to the prayer that is made in this place. ¹⁶ For now I have chosen and consecrated this house that my name may be there forever. My eyes and my heart will be there for all time."

NOTE TO THE TEACHER

Welcome to Renaissance and Revival!

This unit moves through the movers and shakers of the Renaissance—starting in Italy and expanding outward throughout Europe. It is important to note that none of the people we are going to talk about in this unit are perfect. Many artists during this period had at least rumors and accusations that went around regarding their sexuality or morality in general. Today, these rumors are latched onto and there is much conjecture—most of which there is very little proof for. You may want to preview websites and keywords if you are doing additional research. In these lessons we have chosen to stick with facts alone.

When considering this unit and the nature of its depth, I decided not to do color coded sections. Instead, I have aimed to make all content as relevant as possible to all ages with plenty of similes and examples to make things simple and relatable. That being said, this unit is best suited for older students from Upper Elementary and up. While it can be done with the whole family, I would not recommend it for younger students on their own unless they are doing it alongside their older siblings. If you have students who are Early Elementary and younger, save this one for when they are a bit older or take your time with it—breaking it up into smaller sections so it isn't too overwhelming.

Like Life Skills, we have done notebooking a bit more interactively, breaking up the Teacher's Guide lesson with notebooking prompts so that the information is fresh in everyone's minds and notetaking is more spread out and less overwhelming.

While the unit does work loosely chronologically through the Renaissance, it does so in the form of people and their achievements. This means that there is some bouncing around amidst the lessons as we discover the bigger picture of each person's contribution. You will also notice it has a section in each lesson about revivals that are usually in a completely different time period. This is because at its root, the heart of this unit is revival. Revival in art, architecture, thought, education, and religion. We could not talk about reformation of culture and society without seeing the connection of spiritual revivals and the effects they have and so there is a daily detour to focus on random revivals big and small. These focuses replace the family devotional as they are such a recurring theme.

Finally, each day there is a page on Shakespeare and understanding old language. Younger students focus on *thees* and *thous* and break down some quotes as well as relate it to hymns while older students dig a bit deeper. The unit will end with a performance of either a monologue or a skit of some sort, so practice reading out loud with inflection, emotion, and a dramatic flair—especially over a cup of hot tea!

I hope this unit is full of wonder and awe, depth and discovery, and hope and inspiration. May we all be inspired to see the beauty that is all around us in a new way and, above all else, draw closer to the Father in the process.

Love,

Rebecca Spooner

Renaissance and Revival

TABLE OF CONTENTS

FRONT MATTER

NOTE TO THE TEACHER

RECITATION

Lesson 1	Introducing the Renaissance	10
Lesson 2	The Medici Family	15
Lesson 3	Donatello	19
Lesson 4	The Age of Exploration	24
Lesson 5	Leonardo da Vinci	28
Lesson 6	Michelangelo	34
Lesson 7	Raphael	39
Lesson 8	Henry VIII	43
Lesson 9	Desiderius Erasmus	48
Lesson 10	Martin Luther	53
Lesson 11	William Tyndale	58
Lesson 12	Copernicus	62
Lesson 13	Catherine de' Medici	67
Lesson 14	Queen Mary I	73
Lesson 15	Religious Wars	78
Lesson 16	Giorgio Vasari	84
Lesson 17	William Shakespeare	88
Lesson 18	Galileo	92
Lesson 19	King James	96
Lesson 20	Turning the Page	101
Appendix		104
Timeline Cutouts		109

Renaissance and Revival

LESSON 1: INTRODUCING THE RENAISSANCE

As the Middle Ages came to a close, a new dawn was on the horizon. Rapid growth, development, expansion, and advancement happened on nearly every front. Art, architecture, science, mathematics, physics, literature—all aspects of society were launched forward at light speed. After living with the constant companions of war and death, this new era was a welcome relief. The next age would be called the *Renaissance*—which really just means "**revival**" or "awakening." What was dead and thought to be lost forever came back to life in a new way. Throughout this study we'll discover the big ideas of the time as well as some of the key players whose names would go down in history for what they brought to the table. We'll trek across Europe, following the ripple effects of the simple decisions and bold convictions that changed hearts, tore down establishments, and transformed nations. But first let's find out why it happened at all.

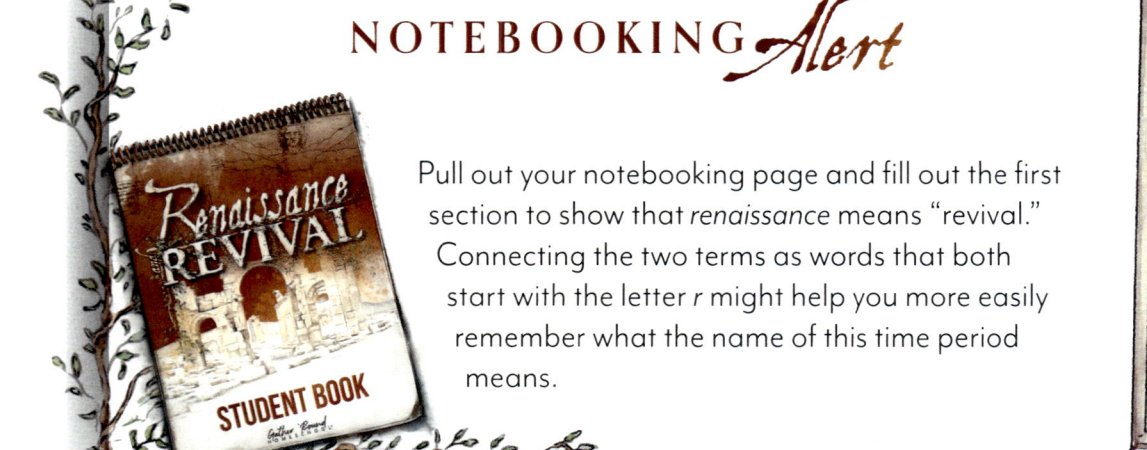

NOTEBOOKING *Alert*

Pull out your notebooking page and fill out the first section to show that *renaissance* means "revival." Connecting the two terms as words that both start with the letter *r* might help you more easily remember what the name of this time period means.

WHAT STARTED IT?

Most big changes start with a new way of thinking. But in the case of the Renaissance, change was actually inspired by the *old*. After centuries of kings and even the church telling them what to do and think, people wanted to be seen and valued for who they were as individuals—and to do this they began to look back toward classic **ideals** from ancient times as well as to philosophers such as Socrates, Plato, and Aristotle. In fact if we peel away all the layers and make it as simple as possible, the Renaissance was kind of like a revival of **philosophy**—something that few had the time for during the devastation of hardships such as the Black Plague. What did it mean to be human? Who were people as individuals? This way of thinking was called *humanism* because of its focus on, well, humans. Many classical writings were lost during the Middle Ages, and the Renaissance was a time for rediscovery and preservation. If it was classical, it was "trending"—and this rise in popularity had a great effect on the culture. Families looked to send their children to schools that followed a more classical model of education. Builders incorporated classic elements like columns into their architecture. Artists tried their hands at new sculptures and paintings by using old styles in new ways. Instead of reinventing the wheel, people went back to build on the work of those before them. With the assistance of the rich and famous and the focus on education, art, and literature . . . it was no wonder that things began to change!

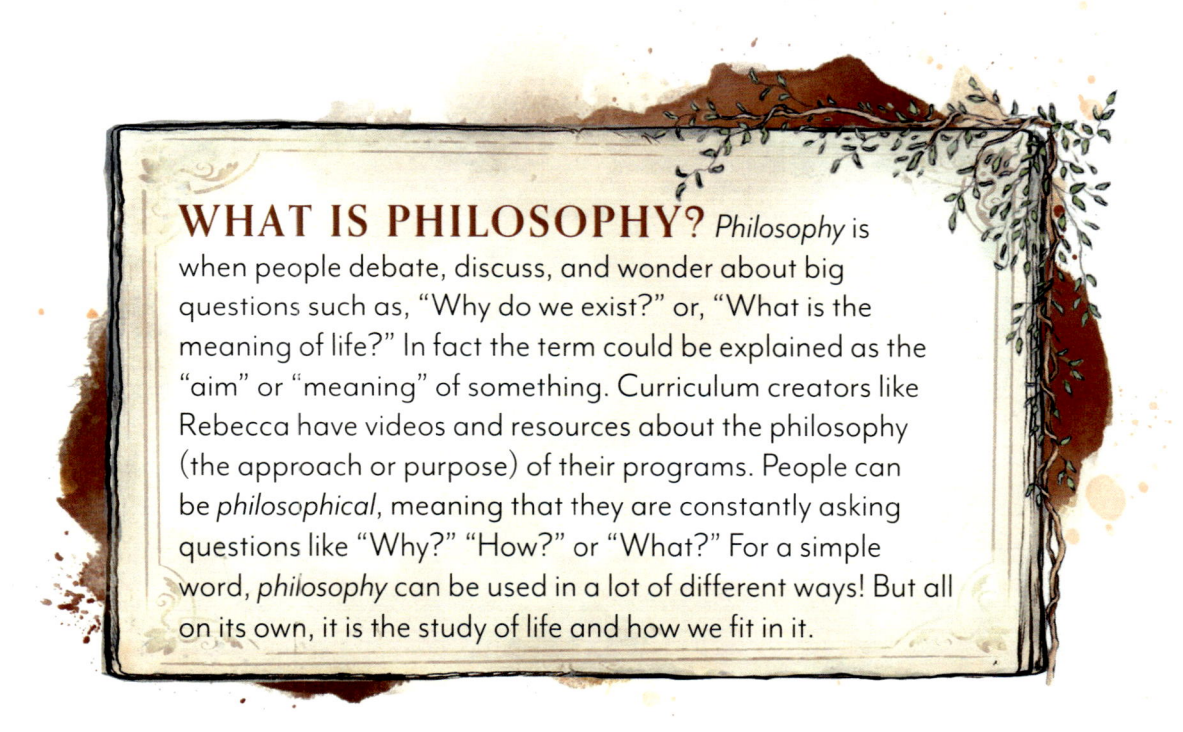

> **WHAT IS PHILOSOPHY?** *Philosophy* is when people debate, discuss, and wonder about big questions such as, "Why do we exist?" or, "What is the meaning of life?" In fact the term could be explained as the "aim" or "meaning" of something. Curriculum creators like Rebecca have videos and resources about the philosophy (the approach or purpose) of their programs. People can be *philosophical*, meaning that they are constantly asking questions like "Why?" "How?" or "What?" For a simple word, *philosophy* can be used in a lot of different ways! But all on its own, it is the study of life and how we fit in it.

WHERE IT ALL BEGAN

Have you ever watched a video of a tsunami? Somewhere out in the middle of the ocean, an earthquake hits and starts a wave that grows ever greater as it approaches land—pushing water where water shouldn't be. We call the place where the earthquake shook the ground the *epicenter*. It is where the earthquake **originated** (or started). In the same way, the Renaissance had an epicenter too. It began in Italy and spread outward like a giant wave, reaching its long arm of progress across Europe like an unstoppable force. Historians have no problem agreeing on the *where*, but the *when* is another story. Do a quick online search about when the Middle Ages ended and the Renaissance began, and you'll find a bunch of different answers. The reality is that these two periods kind of overlap, and the timeline varies depending on certain perspectives and opinions (plus it matters what location you are talking about). Despite the controversy, somewhere around the middle of the 14th century (which, remember, means the 1300s), there was a shift. And this shift would alter the **trajectory** of not just the boot of Italy but all of Europe (and eventually the whole world).

NOTEBOOKING/LAPBOOK *Alert*

Pull out your notebooking page or lapbook and mark Italy on the map to show where the Renaissance started. Then draw ripples (like you would see in the water) going out all across the world to show how it spread.

NOTABLE ARCHITECTURE

If you've ever seen a picture of the Leaning Tower of Pisa, you'll probably know it is famous for its unmistakable tilt. This bell tower was started in the Middle Ages but wasn't completed until about 1372, right around the beginning of the Italian Renaissance. It had columns and arches in Romanesque fashion and was around 186 feet (57 m) tall with eight floors and two spiral staircases inside. After constructing about three floors, the builders realized that the tower was starting to lean. Can you imagine that conversation?

"Hey, wait a minute; is the tower *leaning*?"

"No way! It's just your eyesight, William!"

"I don't think so; look at it from here . . ."

What made it start to tilt? The soil was too soft and therefore unstable! Thankfully war and hardship caused the builders to take a break, which engineers think might have saved the tower from collapse. When construction resumed over a hundred years later, the new engineer tried to **compensate** for the leaning by making the building a bit taller on the other side. But that only made it heavier and caused it to sink even more. Eventually it was finished off, with one of the staircases needing two extra steps to compensate for the angle. By the 20th century, the leaning was so bad that the tower was shut down for repairs. To help stabilize the building, they removed a bunch of dirt from underneath it, causing a reduction in the angle and making it safe for tourists for a few more centuries. So what can we learn from this colossal mistake? Today engineers take soil samples and assess foundations to make sure a new construction won't sink. It might have felt like a failure, but we are left with one of the most sought after tourist destinations and some important lessons learned . . . so maybe it wasn't a total loss.

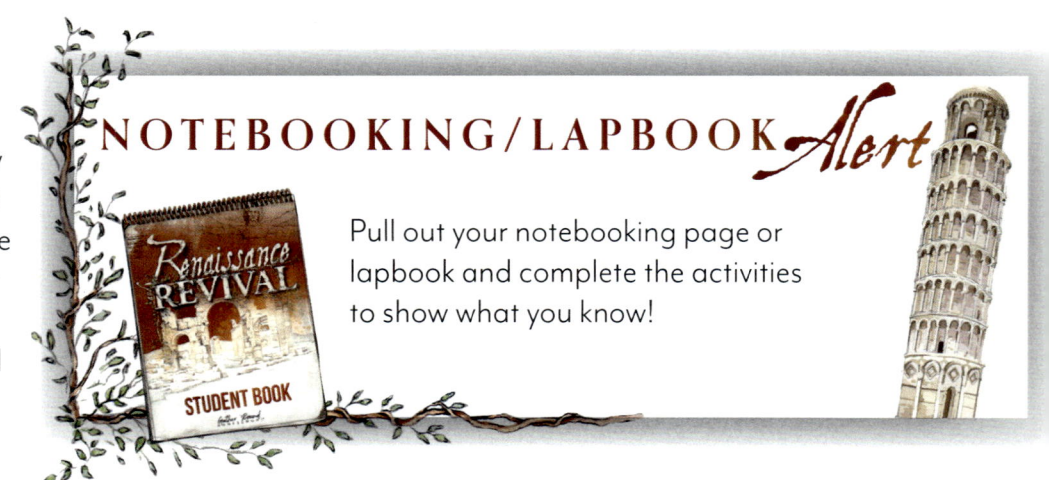

NOTEBOOKING/LAPBOOK *Alert*

Pull out your notebooking page or lapbook and complete the activities to show what you know!

TEACHER'S GUIDE LESSON 1 INTRODUCING THE RENAISSANCE

REVIVAL IS IN THE AIR

If you completed our study on the Middle Ages, you might recall that the church played a big part in politics and culture. Humanism was kind of like an overcorrection of that, focusing on people, personal development, and abilities instead of the establishment of the church as a whole. Have you ever heard the phrase, "I feel like I'm just a number"? In large organizations (like the government or a megachurch) it's easy to feel a bit lost or like no one knows you. People probably don't know your name because you're just one in a sea of many . . . adding to the overall numbers but meaning very little. This is kind of how people felt after the control of popes and kings, and they were hungry for something more personal. Some wanted nothing to do with the church. They were weary of being controlled and limited. But others saw the problem and wanted to help fix it. Religion had become little more than tradition for most—an impersonal tribute to a disconnected God. But the scriptures were full of passages that said otherwise! God was a friend to Moses.[1] Jesus said that He knew how many hairs were on our heads.[2] Jeremiah declared that God had a plan and a purpose.[3] People were longing for meaning, direction, and a sense of value . . . and some reformers believed that a personal relationship with God was not only possible but necessary.

In this unit we will also be studying revivals that may have not all happened during this time period but which were like little renaissances all on their own, affecting entire neighborhoods, towns, cities, regions, and even nations! We'll tour the globe, learning about events big and small where people encountered our personal God in a very personal way. Our study of this time period (and beyond) is one of hope. In the middle of our torn and often dark-feeling world, God can bring new life, beauty from the ashes, healing to what is broken, and unity to what is impossibly divided . . . and we're about to see that proven time and time again. He is the designer of every good and perfect gift—our brilliant ideas and genius discoveries. He is the inspirer of beauty, the author of creativity, and the usherer of the new. "Behold, I am doing a new thing; now it springs forth, do you not perceive it? I will make a way in the wilderness and rivers in the desert"—Isaiah 43:19. Revival, my friend, is in the air! Grab hold of it and see what the transformative power of God can do—how it can send out ripples from the epicenter of your heart.

HANDS-ON *Activity*

Constructing a tower is no small feat! A building has to be carefully planned to make sure that the foundation can support it. Try making a tower of your own. You can use blocks, rocks, bricks, sticks, or anything else. See who can build their tower the tallest. Don't forget to start with a solid foundation!

VOCABULARY

EARLY READER
revival: *a change to make something better or new again*
ideal: *something that is considered to be perfect*

EARLY ELEMENTARY
ideal: *something that is considered to be perfect*
compensate: *to correct something in order to make it equal*

UPPER ELEMENTARY
compensate: *to correct something in order to make it equal*
philosophy: *the study of life and how we fit in it*

MIDDLE SCHOOL
philosophy: *the study of life and how we fit in it*
trajectory: *the path that something follows*

HIGH SCHOOL
trajectory: *the path that something follows*
originate: *to start*

Renaissance and Revival

LESSON 2: THE MEDICI FAMILY

Imagine that your parents had no home for you to live in, no job to earn money, no food to put on the table, and no ability to teach you how to read, write, or do basic math. To grow up in extreme **poverty** would be like standing at the bottom of a ladder. You have nowhere to go but up, yet there is a long way to climb in order to get pretty much anything and everything you need. Now think about your own life. Does one (or both) of your parents have a job? Do you live in a house? Do you get to learn how to read and write? Your starting point—what feels like the bottom of the ladder to you—might be the very top for someone else. While any person can climb to amazing heights and achieve amazing things when they work hard and persevere, not everyone is given the same opportunities—nor do they start off at the same spots. Things were no different at the beginning of the Renaissance. Some children were born into wealthy families that owned land, held **prestigious** positions, had a lot of money, and were well respected in their communities and cities. One such family was the Medici family—theirs was a name that carried weight and meaning. Let's pop over for a visit!

NEW OPPORTUNITY

There's something about packing up your family and going somewhere new. No one knows who you are. It's like wiping the slate clean and starting fresh. You might be at the bottom of the ladder, but everything that is before you is full of possibilities—there are no limits! This is precisely what happened to the Medicis. They left their home and moved to the city-state of Florence, Italy, in the 12th century. Starting off as merchants, they bought and sold goods, climbing the ladder rung by rung. Their progress was passed down like a birthright to their sons and daughters. As they built their personal **wealth**, they dabbled in banking as well. By the end of the 13th century, the Medicis were a force to be reckoned with, and everyone knew their name—even though they weren't nobility like the other powerful families in the city. They became head of the merchant guild, were involved in politics, and started their own bank: *the Medici Bank*. Over the next hundred years, this bank would continue to build and grow, becoming the leading institution in the area and making the Medici family one of the most powerful families in Florence. If we trace the aftershock waves of the Renaissance back to their source, the epicenter was actually right here in Florence! And an undeniable trigger was none other than a single family who had taken the risk of a new beginning.

TEACHER'S GUIDE LESSON 2 — THE MEDICI FAMILY

NOTEBOOKING/LAPBOOK Alert

Pull out your notebooking page and fill out section one to show what kinds of things the Medicis had influence over. Then find Florence and label Italy on the map.

TWO GREAT RULERS

Many generations of Medicis contributed to the family's success, but there are two members who were **arguably** the most influential, loved, and remembered: Cosimo and his grandson Lorenzo. Cosimo may not have been a king, but he ruled like one. A shrewd politician who made wise decisions that kept people happy and unified, he also had a great love for art and literature and invested large sums of money toward this aim. In fact, he became friends with many architects and artists who he **commissioned** to do work within the city. His love for literature led him to search for ancient manuscripts and put them together in a library. He paid people to copy the manuscripts so the works could be restored and used for learning—he even translated all of the writings of Plato. During his time in power, Cosimo was able to secure his family's position for the next century while making great leaps forward on nearly every front in the city. When he died in 1464, a huge procession attended his funeral, where he was lovingly remembered as Pater Patriae ("Father of His Country").

After Cosimo's successful rule, his younger son Piero took his place. Piero was weak and sickly. He died only five years after taking power, passing the baton on to his son (Cosimo's grandson) Lorenzo. Like his grandfather, Lorenzo had a knack for leadership and a love for art, education, and history. He was only 20 years old when his father died, making his successful rule all the more extraordinary. He seemed to have a knack for politics, and his charming personality made him beloved by all. As you might have discovered by now in your own life, none of us can be good at *everything*, and Lorenzo was no exception. He might have had a politician's mind, but he did more spending than saving. Under his rule the Medici Bank started to go downhill. He poured finances toward his passions of art and literature, which was a big help when it came to the Renaissance, but it would have lasting effects for his family's enterprises.

LORENZO DE' MEDICI

He opened the Medici library to the public and was a proud supporter of some of the greats in the art world: Michelangelo, Leonardo, and Botticelli. He would go down in the history books as Lorenzo the Magnificent. With the help of the Medicis, Florence was the site of a cultural shaking—and no one had any idea just how far this shaking would spread.

NOTEBOOKING/LAPBOOK Alert

Pull out your timeline (either in your appendix or in the lapbook) and add the figures for Cosimo and Lorenzo.

TEACHER'S GUIDE LESSON 2

THE MEDICI FAMILY

NOTABLE ART

If you've ever heard the saying, "Those who can't do, teach,"[4] you might assume that the Medici family's passion for the arts came from the outside looking in—they loved it because they weren't good at it themselves. Lorenzo, however, was a highly creative person who **dabbled** in poetry. His enthusiasm and appreciation for art and literature made him place high value on not just works but also on the artists themselves. This drew creators from far and wide. Like singers and musicians who travel to Nashville (Music City), hoping that they will find fame, or actors who go to Hollywood seeking their big break, artists found a home in Florence. Word started to get around that there was money, work, and a community in Italy. Aspiring artists, sculptors, architects, and poets would come to work under those who were masters in their field. Talent and creativity was cultivated not only because of patrons like Lorenzo but because of the emphasis that a shifting culture placed on the arts. And it was here in Florence that some of the world's most beautiful pieces were created. Take a look below at the painting by Andrea Mantegna, an Italian painter who lived around the same time as Lorenzo. What do you notice about it? Where is your eye drawn first? Artists often use light, shadow, and detail to draw an observer's attention to what is most important in the scene they have created. In this painting the man in yellow (who is supposed to be Joseph) is the key player, an exhausted new father resting after a long trip and probably long night. If you look closely, the shepherds look bedraggled with torn clothing and holes in their shoes (or no shoes at all). They look like they ran straight from the field! Mantegna was probably only about 20 years old when he painted this scene—a result of having been raised up in the presence of greatness.

THE ADORATION OF THE SHEPHERDS BY ANDREA MANTEGNA

NOTEBOOKING/LAPBOOK *Alert*

Pull out your notebooking page and color or paint the painting. Where will you put light and shadow? Where do you want the focus to be? If you are doing a lapbook instead, add the painting to the Renaissance Museum.

TEACHER'S GUIDE LESSON 2   **THE MEDICI FAMILY**

THE PROTESTANT REFORMATION

Humanism came about in part as a reaction to the strict control of and dependency on the church, as there were some who thought that things should be different. We'll hear more about some of these reformers in a later lesson. But it helps to have an overall understanding of Protestant vs. Catholic beliefs. After Jesus came, His disciples spread out, sharing the gospel far and wide. Before their deaths they set up churches and leaders, and it was these leaders who took over telling people about Jesus. Eventually the Catholic Church was established as *the* church. You were either a part of it or you were considered a pagan. During the Renaissance, the Protestant Reformation challenged many points of Catholic theology and doctrine. Protestants disagreed with people buying indulgences for the forgiveness of their sins. They did not believe that someone needed to go through a priest or the pope for their sins but could rather go directly to God themselves. These debates were important, but it was a long and bloody battle toward peace. For many years extreme views on both sides meant persecution no matter what you believed or who you agreed with. The church was fractured and broken, with people following different reformers with different viewpoints. This is where many of our denominations come from. But it was from these cracks and broken places that many amazing revivals were birthed as well. In the same way that the Medici family was at the epicenter of change that spread all across Europe, the Protestant Reformation was at the epicenter of the revivals that would spread in waves across the whole world. Time and time again, people's limited views about God were challenged, and their theology was shaken by the new thing He was doing. This is why we're studying revivals even though their dates might not match up with the Renaissance—they were like aftershocks of change, each with their own impacts, spreading like contagions that could not be stopped.

VOCABULARY

EARLY READER
poverty: *when someone does not have enough money to buy what they need*
wealth: *a large amount of money and belongings*

EARLY ELEMENTARY
wealth: *a large amount of money and belongings*
prestigious: *respected and admired by people*

UPPER ELEMENTARY
prestigious: *respected and admired by people*
arguably: *easily proven to be true*

MIDDLE SCHOOL
arguably: *easily proven to be true*
dabble: *to take part in something in a small, unofficial way*

HIGH SCHOOL
dabble: *to take part in something in a small, unofficial way*
commission: *payment and request for a job to be done*

HANDS-ON *Activity*

Run a race but have every person start at a different spot. Place one person much farther ahead, the smallest person the farthest back, etc.—creating unfair advantages and disadvantages. Start the race, see who wins, and then talk about how we can have different opportunities in our lives and have to make the best of what we have been given. Tie in Romans 12:3–8 and Luke 12:48. What kind of privileges and opportunities do you have? Discuss beauty/looks, economic status, and even spiritual legacy (the privilege of being raised in God's word vs. someone who doesn't find Jesus until much later in life). Then take some time to be thankful.

Renaissance and Revival

LESSON 3: DONATELLO

If you were to go to the library and search for books about the Renaissance, you might find that some titles are confusing. Because it was such a long period, many organize the Renaissance by time, using identifying words such as early, high, late, proto, and so forth. Others prefer to look at this period as a flame-like torch that was passed from person to person and place to place. Instead of using time, these people categorize the Renaissance's progression by *region*, such as the *Northern Renaissance*. The Early Renaissance started in Italy, so this term refers to a similar period of time known as the *Italian Renaissance*—when art and literature were like snowballs rolling downhill, gaining both momentum and strength. If you think of the Medicis being similar to famous people in Hollywood, things start to make a bit more sense. Their power was not just related to their money, it was also heavily reliant on their influence. What they did, people followed. And their focus on literature and the arts triggered others to concentrate on the same things. For the first time in a while, art was sustainable. Instead of having a grueling job and doing art on the side, artists were commissioned and paid for their work, allowing them the opportunity to become masters at their crafts. Today we're going to look at one of the Early Renaissance artists who was a **pioneer** in the sculpting world. So pull out your chisel and let's walk in the footsteps of the great Donatello.

SAINT MARK BY DONATELLO

TEACHER'S GUIDE LESSON 3   **DONATELLO**

THE LIFE AND TIMES

Donatello (whose real name was actually Donato di Niccolo di Betto Bardi) was born in 1386 in the epicenter of Florence. Not much is known about his early life other than the fact that his father was a wool carder—which meant that he combed wool to remove the tangles and to get it ready to be spun. One of the only childhood records that has stood the test of time is the story of a fight that Donatello got into when he was about 15 years old, hitting someone on the head with a club (ouch). We can **deduce** that he had a keen interest in art by the fact that he was an apprentice at the age of only 18. He spent a lot of time studying ancient and classical sculptures in both form and style. Donatello specialized in sculpting with different mediums including marble, bronze, clay, and even wood! It didn't take long until his name was recognized, and he was being hired for projects of his own. He **emulated** the classical style of ancient Greece and Rome but with a new sense of realism that was highly appealing during this humanistic era. He paid attention to perspective, angles, expressions, and even anatomy, making god-like saints and figures look altogether human and vulnerable. He started off by sculpting biblical figures—such as the prophet Jeremiah and St. John the Baptist—for churches, each sculpture taking him years to complete. Can you imagine working that long on one piece of art?

It's no surprise that Cosimo de' Medici took notice of Donatello's rising talent and became one of his greatest supporters and even his friend. Under Cosimo's protection Donatello was free to pursue mastery in his craft without having to worry about upsetting his patrons. He was said to have been quite particular with a fiery personality. He not only cared deeply about his art but also about where it went and how it was portrayed. He was willing to break his work into pieces rather than have it go to someone he didn't like. In the end it was Cosimo himself who commissioned Donatello's most famous sculpture: a bronze statue of David that was quite controversial at the time, mainly because it was completely nude. While nude art wasn't uncommon in ancient times, it hadn't been done in many centuries, and there had never been a biblical figure portrayed this way before. Donatello died of unknown causes in 1466 when he was about 80 years old, but not before paving the way for other artists who would be inspired by the liberties he had taken and the styles he had revived and renewed. Picking up his baton of progress, what new pieces would be birthed by other artists throughout the Renaissance? Only time would tell.

NOTEBOOKING/LAPBOOK *Alert*

Pull out your timeline (either in your appendix or in the lapbook) and add the figure for Donatello.

NOTABLE ART

Arguably Donatello's most famous piece of art was his bronze sculpture of David. This groundbreaking statue was a big deal for a few reasons. First of all, Donatello was the first sculptor since ancient times to make a freestanding nude statue. Freestanding meant that they had no support from a wall or another structure. We've already talked about the shocking move that Donatello made by **depicting** one of the most beloved Bible characters of all time in the nude—his throwback to the classical period of ancient history. But the style of art was another thing entirely. The David statue was in a position called *contrapposto*—where the subject is leaning its weight on one foot. This was another technique that hadn't been used since ancient Greece and made David appear more realistic and natural—pioneering a new path for the artists who would follow. The idea of young David triumphing over the giant, Goliath, was also a symbol near and dear to Florence's heart. It might have been only a small city-state, but it was wealthy and strong—able to stand up to the larger areas around it. Take a look at the sculpture here (with our blur effect added) and talk about what makes it unique and different. What do you like or not like about it?

NOTEBOOKING/LAPBOOK *Alert*

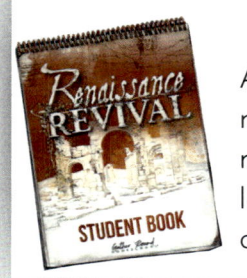

Add the statue of David to your notebooking page or lapbook museum and write some things you learned or your own observations about it.

MEANWHILE IN THE REST OF THE WORLD

Right around the time that Donatello was busy sculpting his bronze depiction of David's triumph over Goliath, an amazing invention was being born over in Germany. A metalsmith named Johannes Gutenberg was struggling in his business and decided to try something new—a modern printing press. First he had to cast metal letters. He made molds to pour the metal into and then plates to **affix** them to. Next he had to formulate his own ink—it had to be able to stick to metal, something that the ink of the time didn't naturally do. Finally he had to find a way to make paper thinner so that it would go through the press easier. He did this by using an old winepress to flatten the paper so it would run through smoothly. He might have had a talent for working with metal, but ink and paper were not his specialties. It would take him 10 years to figure out all of the parts and to perfect his invention, but by 1450 the Gutenberg press was complete—and it would change everything. The renaissance that had started in Italy would now be able to spread much more quickly. Books could be printed and distributed, ideas could be shared, and the Bible could get into the hands of the common man. The Renaissance wasn't the result of any one person, idea, or action; rather, it was the outcome of a bunch of dominoes all playing their parts in the season they were in, propelling their world forward in one way or another. They had been born for such a time as this, and one by one, they would spread outward in an incredible display for us to see.

DAVID STATUE BY DONATELLO

NOTEBOOKING/LAPBOOK Alert

Pull out your notebook or lapbook and complete the section about the Gutenberg press. What about it stood out to you the most?

KIRK OF SHOTTS REVIVAL

After the Protestant Reformation, Europe was in religious turmoil. There seemed to be more disagreements than unity, and fear, judgment, and even persecution were common. Under the surface however, people like Robert Bruce, a minister, were moved to pray for change. Little did they know that their prayers were about to be answered. One fine day two wealthy women were traveling when their carriage broke down near a town called Shotts (in Scotland). The malfunction was no accident, however, as God had a divine meeting planned for them. A local minister helped to repair the carriage and hosted the ladies while it was being fixed. Upon entering the man's home, the women saw that it was in poor condition and offered to build a new house for the church. Have you ever heard the passage, " . . . Outdo one another in showing honor" (Romans 12:10b)? The minister was incredibly moved by the generosity of these travelers and asked what he could do for them in return. The women asked for but one thing: "Let us put on a special church service and allow us to choose who will lead it." They invited Robert Bruce and other leaders to conduct the service, and on Sunday, June 20, 1630 . . . the people gathered.

But this was no ordinary service. There were far too many people to fit in the small parish, so the crowds gathered outside. Those who were there experienced a supernatural sense of peace and joy, and they didn't want to leave. They ended up staying overnight and into the next day, **interceding** for the lost and talking passionately about God. On Monday morning a young man named John Livingstone (who was not ordained yet) was asked to speak. Imagine it. You're young, not even officially a minister, and surrounded by about 1,000 people—some who have far more experience speaking than you do! The presence of God was tangible, and John was nervous, insecure, and full of doubt. He agreed to speak but then had second thoughts and walked out of the building, continuing on until the church was almost out of sight. But the Lord had other plans. He wasn't looking for the most experienced or the most eloquent speaker; He just needed someone who was available. God stopped John in his tracks, speaking to him, "Was I ever a barren wilderness, or a land of darkness?" The young man returned to the pulpit, no less afraid but unable to disobey God's call. He preached a sermon of power based on Ezekiel 36:25–26, "I will sprinkle clean water on you, and you shall be clean from all your uncleannesses, and from all your idols I will cleanse you . . . " In heavenly timing, rain began to fall, and people were so convicted of their sin—cut to the heart—that many fell over, and 500 people turned to Jesus. Antique, dead religion awakened to a real, vibrant relationship with the King of Kings . . . a renaissance of the human heart.

TEACHER'S GUIDE LESSON 3 — DONATELLO

EXTENSION Activity

Read a portion of the sermon that John preached in the appendix and talk about it as a family. Have you ever experienced conviction like that?

HANDS-ON Activity

The first printing press worked kind of like a stamp. It had raised letters that could be moved to make words that were then pressed onto paper. Try making your own stamp! You could pour wax into dough to see how molds were made or try to carve a shape into an apple, banana, or potato and then dip it in paint. If you'd rather, try making your own sculpture out of dough or clay instead. Do you think it would be easier to work with a moldable medium like clay or a hard medium like rock that had to be carved? Why?

VOCABULARY

EARLY READER
pioneer: *a person who is the first to explore a new area or start a new trend*
affix: *to stick or attach to something*

EARLY ELEMENTARY
affix: *to stick or attach to something*
deduce: *to come to a conclusion or understanding about something*

UPPER ELEMENTARY
deduce: *to come to a conclusion or understanding about something*
emulate: *to try to copy someone or something*

MIDDLE SCHOOL
emulate: *to try to copy someone or something*
depict: *to portray in words or art*

HIGH SCHOOL
depict: *to portray in words or art*
intercede: *to pray on behalf of someone*

Renaissance and Revival

LESSON 4: THE AGE OF EXPLORATION

The Renaissance wasn't just about art and literature—it was also like a propeller urging people to learn, grow, and make a name for themselves. While most citizens in Florence were focused on politics, art, and philosophy, there were some who dreamed of making their marks in different ways. These explorers had big ideas about the world, and the only way to test these beliefs was to get into ships and see where the currents of the sea would lead. But in the same way that an art sculpture could take years to finish and often depended on financial support, exploring was an even more expensive **venture**. Unlike an artist who usually just needed a few materials to complete their work, exploration required an entire crew of men and a very costly ship full of supplies. Before one could make their mark, therefore, they needed to have **buy-in** from the rich and wealthy. Today we'll take a closer look at a few of the adventurers who experienced a renaissance of cartography, geography, and science. Curiosity would be awakened and revived, and it was about to fill the world with wonder and awe!

NOTEBOOKING/LAPBOOK Alert

Color or sketch a ship while you listen to the lesson. As you do so, think about how ships, exploration, and even travel has changed over the centuries.

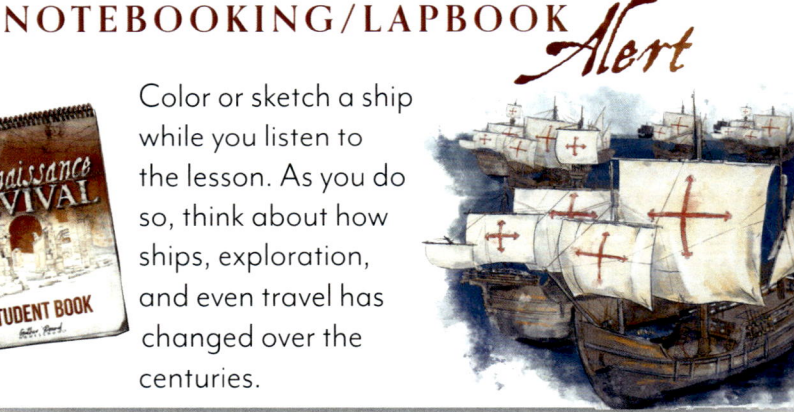

NEW ROUTES OR NEW LANDS?

Have you ever heard or read the poem "In 1492"? This piece of literature talks about the explorer Christopher Columbus, and it is a helpful way to remember what year he went on his first voyage. Columbus was born in 1451 to wool weavers who lived in a port town in Italy. He grew up watching the ships coming in and out of port, and it wasn't long before he got his first job at sea. By the time he was about 20 years old, Columbus was an **avid** sailor. Contrary to popular belief, he didn't actually have **grandiose** ideas of sailing around the world. Rather, he wanted to find new trade routes to the Far East in order to help merchants like his parents. He traveled all the way to Portugal when he was around the age of 25 to seek supporters for his vision. It would take him nearly 16 years to finally convince the king and queen of Spain to "come on board" with his plan. And at last in 1492, his hard work paid off when he and his 90 sailors set sail on the Atlantic aboard their small fleet of three ships.

TEACHER'S GUIDE LESSON 4   THE AGE OF EXPLORATION

EXTENSION *Activity*

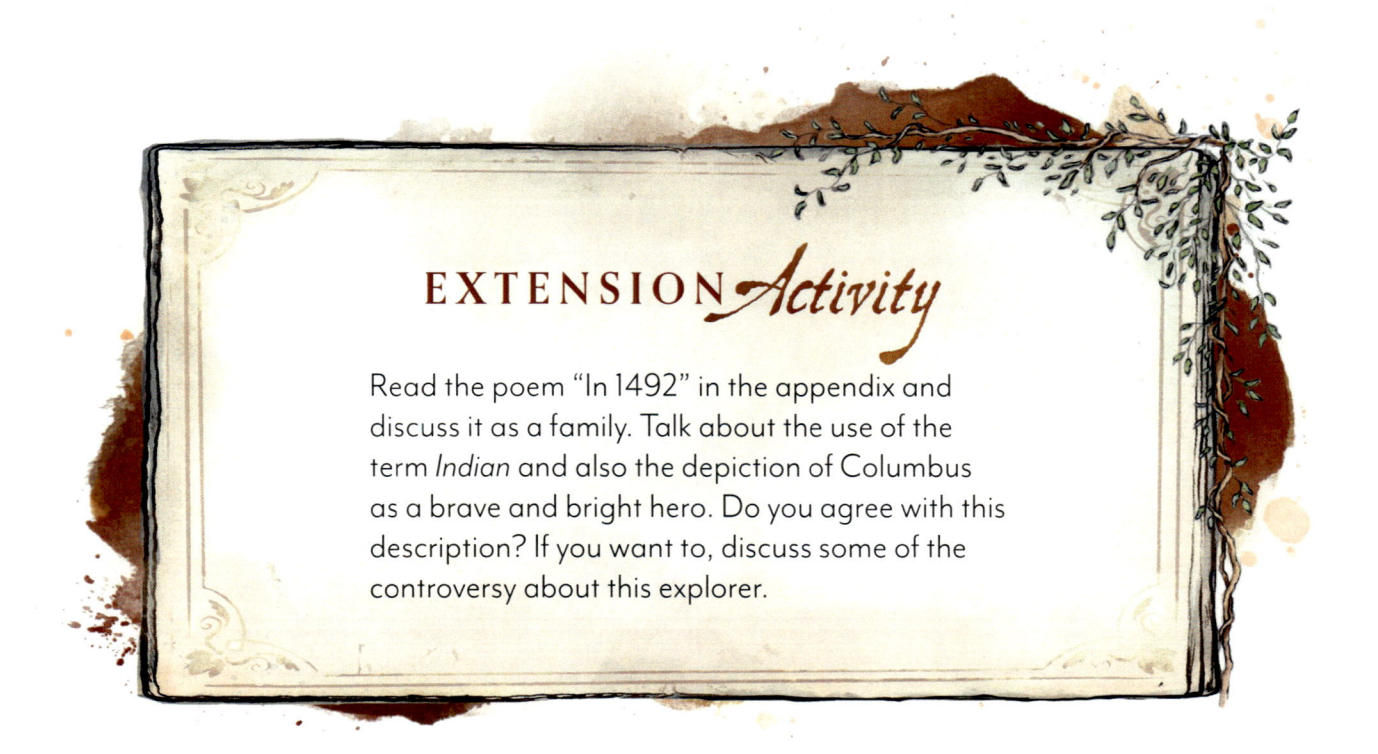

Read the poem "In 1492" in the appendix and discuss it as a family. Talk about the use of the term *Indian* and also the depiction of Columbus as a brave and bright hero. Do you agree with this description? If you want to, discuss some of the controversy about this explorer.

Columbus never actually made it to the United States of America. What he called the "New World" was really the Bahamas and later parts of Central and South America. It was the explorer who came after him that really "made waves" in the water as a part of the first expedition to **circumnavigate** (or sail around) the world—though he himself wouldn't make it all the way. Ferdinand Magellan was born to wealthy nobles in Portugal in 1480. When his parents died, he became a page in the queen's court in Lisbon, but he dreamed of the sea as he heard heroic stories of sailing, battles, and discoveries. After getting his sea legs while traveling on trade routes, he never looked back. Like Columbus, Magellan wanted to expand sailing routes and knew that the king of Spain would want to corner the spice market. Ferdinand sailed there in hopes of getting a sponsor, and he was successful, soon heading west across the Atlantic with five ships stocked full of supplies. The trip would prove to be costly and the necessities not enough. The crews would battle scurvy, survive a mutiny, run critically low on food and water, get involved in battles, and lose ships to storms, returning home about three years later with only one of the five vessels left. Magellan himself lost his life after getting involved in a battle between two chieftains, but the cat was out of the bag . . . the world was a lot bigger than anyone had guessed.

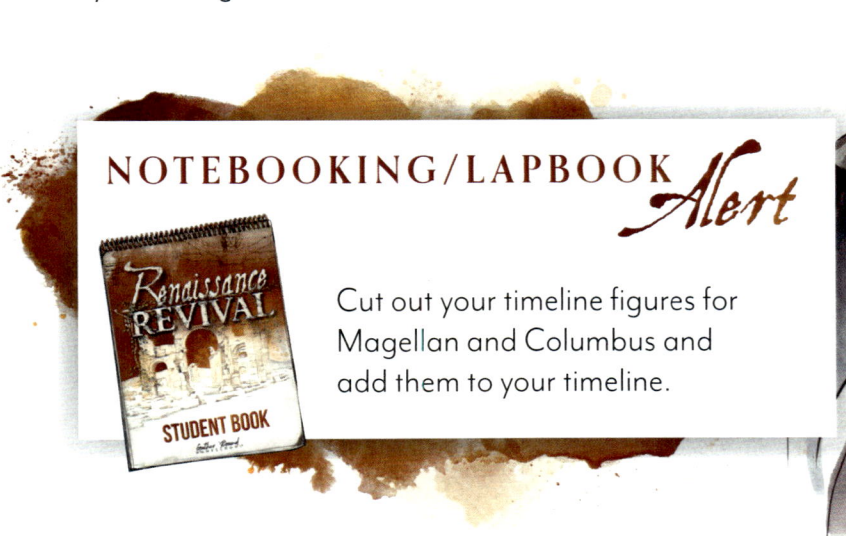

NOTEBOOKING/LAPBOOK *Alert*

Cut out your timeline figures for Magellan and Columbus and add them to your timeline.

NOTABLE SCIENCE

It must have been quite scary to sail into the great unknown. Right before Columbus left, a globe of the world had been made, but it didn't show any of North or South America, as they had not been discovered yet. The Age of Exploration was like the starter gun of a race. Once it went off, the sense of adventure was nearly **palpable**. New land meant new possibilities. Sailors and wannabe sailors alike began to dream of what discovering territories might mean for them. Could they make a name for themselves? Like during the space race, different countries began mustering their ships and resources to send off expeditions of their own. Men knew that they might not be the very first to circumnavigate the globe, but they could be the first Italian, German, etc., to do so. Exploration, it turned out, was quite scientific. Distances had to be measured, new maps had to be drawn, and locations had to be precise in order to help sailors navigate in uncharted waters. They didn't have GPSs, radars, or any apps. All of their calculations had to be done through math and science—and they used angles to figure out a lot of it. A special tool called an *astrolabe* was also used, which was basically a wheel with two pinholes on either end of an arrow. Navigators would hold it up and look through one side of the arrow to find Polaris, or the North Star. This would tell them the angle from the star to the horizon, giving them their *latitude* (or how far north or south they were). These measurements helped to keep them on straight lines and showed them how far they had gone when they went around land (like South America). By putting all of this information together, sailors started mapping out how big different landmasses were. And even without sophisticated technology, the first accurate world maps were able to be drawn!

ASTROLABE

NOTEBOOKING/LAPBOOK *Alert*

Pull out your notebooking page or lapbook and complete the section for navigation to show what you learned.

MEET THE MORAVIANS

Amazing things were happening in Scotland and Ireland as God's Spirit moved hearts to repentance. Huge crowds gathered, and many gave their lives to Jesus, forever changed by His love. But not all revivals looked like this. Today we will travel to a small village in Germany to see another outpouring that would have very different results. It all started with Nicolaus Zinzendorf, a wealthy young man with a large estate. As the clash between the Protestant and Catholic church heated up, people began to flee persecution. One group of these refugees was the Moravians, who were from an area that is known today as the Czech Republic. Nicolaus built a town for them to settle in, and over 200 gathered there during the next five years. As is often the case with people, it didn't take long for division to break out—especially when it came to beliefs. The villagers argued about doctrine and theology, and it got so bad that Nicolaus drafted up a peace accord called the *Brotherly Agreement* to help the people of the community focus on their similarities rather than their differences. He preached sermons on unity, and the dynamics began to change. The townspeople were no longer fighting, but they still struggled to be united in love. But all that was about to change.

TEACHER'S GUIDE LESSON 4 — THE AGE OF EXPLORATION

In the summer of 1727, only a few months after the agreement was signed, there was a shift. Gatherings were more focused and intentional, and people felt drawn to pray together—sometimes all night. When an 11-year-old girl was compelled to pray for three days, she encountered God in an incredible way, and her story inspired other children in the community. This wasn't just a revival for adults! Church services were electric with the power and the presence of the Lord. On August 13, 1727, the Holy Spirit fell on the entire population in something they would later term the *Moravian Pentecost*. Not one single person in the community was left out. Even those who were out of town or working felt the supernatural presence of the Lord at the exact same moment as their brethren. There were great signs and wonders—though the Moravians never described publicly exactly what those were. Their focus was not on the wonders as much as it was on the love that they felt—for and from God and for one another. This revival would last for 13 days, with the entire village swept up in what God was doing. It was not uncommon to see children kneeling in the bushes or by the side of the road praying, weeping, or crying out to the Lord. The result? Nicolaus felt called to start a 24/7 prayer movement, which would last for 100 years. Both adults and children took different shifts around the clock, praying without ceasing either on their own or in groups of two and three. They prayed for the gospel to be spread and for God's kingdom to be expanded. It was from this well of prayer that the first large-scale missions movement was born. The Moravians would send over 100 missionaries around the world—spreading the fire that had been poured out on them across all of the nations (even America)! One group even felt led to sell themselves into slavery in order to reach lost slaves. Like the ripple effect of the Renaissance that would spread out from Italy, the faithfulness of the Moravians would impact entire generations yet to come. During this time, their church wrote thousands of songs that the people would memorize and sing with perfect accord. The Moravian church never attracted thousands of people. It was not a stadium movement—in fact it never grew above 300 people. It was a slow burn that was carefully stewarded from one generation to the next . . . like the fire at the altar in God's temple—constantly tended to and stoked so it would not burn out.

For this reason I remind you to fan into flame the gift of God, which is in you through the laying on of my hands.
—2 Timothy 1:6

VOCABULARY

EARLY READER
venture: *a plan that could be risky*
avid: *very eager or interested*

EARLY ELEMENTARY
avid: *very eager or interested*
grandiose: *ambitious; over the top*

UPPER ELEMENTARY
grandiose: *ambitious; over the top*
buy-in: *willingness to support someone or something*

MIDDLE SCHOOL
buy-in: *willingness to support someone or something*
circumnavigate: *to travel all the way around something*

HIGH SCHOOL
circumnavigate: *to travel all the way around something*
palpable: *able to be felt*

HANDS-ON *Activity*

New things can be scary, but they are also exciting. Go on an adventure as a family to do something new. You could try out a new restaurant, go to the roller rink, check out a park, or hike a trail that you haven't been on before. As you do the activity, think about how it feels. Are you someone who likes to experience new things, or is it hard for you? How do you feel afterward?

Renaissance and Revival

LESSON 5: LEONARDO DA VINCI

Take a look at the top of this page. Do you notice the drawings and scribbles? Have you ever seen that sketch of a man before? Called the *Vitruvian Man*, it is actually a drawing from Leonardo da Vinci's notebook. Over the years it has become almost a universal symbol for the Renaissance, which is ironic when you consider the fact that its illustrator wasn't really recognized by many of his peers at the time. Leonardo didn't fit the mold or seem to play by the same rules. He wasn't interested in political gain or in making a name for himself. He had an **insatiable** thirst for knowledge, a tender love for God's creation, and a brilliant mind that seemed to have no limitations. Yet despite the fact that he didn't quite fit in during his own time, 500 years later his works are like seasonings in a stew—flavoring the whole pot. Let's take a walk in the footsteps of a true Renaissance man . . . Leonardo da Vinci.

LEONARDO DA VINCI'S EARLY LIFE

Leonardo was born in the small town of Vinci in 1452, though his parents were not married. When he was still young, his mother left, leaving little Leo to be raised by his father and grandmother. From a young age, it was clear that Leonardo was different. He didn't play like other boys did, as he found their games too rough. He spent much of his time in the forest, observing the animals and plants; he was seemingly quite content to be left alone. As is often the case, people who don't do what is expected of them stick out like sore thumbs, and Leonardo was no exception. The townspeople started talking, wondering what was wrong with him and gossipping about him (as people tend to do). When he was seven years old, he was sent to school, but he found himself quite bored with Latin and grammar, and he would skip classes to roam the hills. When he got older and started to learn geometry, his interest was **piqued**, and he showed real promise. At the same time, he discovered music and taught himself how to play multiple instruments. He seemed to be good at anything he tried, and the rumors continued to spread about this boy who stood apart from his peers.

One day his father showed Leonardo's paintings to a famous artist who unsurprisingly scooped him up, saying he had unprecedented talent. For a while Leonardo painted under this master—whose name was Verrocchio—but he didn't seem to need the lessons! Verrocchio grew frustrated with his young pupil who seemed to want to know everything about everything. While most artists had a natural gifting with a particular artform (like sculpting or painting), Leonardo wanted to do them all. He seemed to jump from one project to the next, intent more on the learning than the finishing. One day Verrocchio told his rising star to do something useful—paint him an angel. Leonardo picked up the brush and without a single sketch, plan, or thought, he produced something something far better than Verrocchio ever could have. The rest of the students crowded around. It was like the apprentice had completed a math problem without showing any of his work—everyone was dumbfounded! Verrocchio himself was so blown away that some said he vowed never to paint again (though no one knows if this is a myth or not). The other pupils studied Leonardo's work, perhaps wondering how he had done it so they could try to **replicate** it for themselves. But as his peers looked at his art, the boy quietly slipped out of the room—completely disinterested in the others' praise or attention. It would appear that Leonardo cared more for the knowledge than for the product—he sought the experience over the **acclaim**. He was even known to spend his money on birds just so he could release them from their cages to their freedom. Are you starting to see why he didn't fit in?

NOTEBOOKING/LAPBOOK Alert

Add the timeline figure for Leonardo da Vinci to your timeline.

LATER LIFE

Do you remember Lorenzo the Magnificent? He started commissioning Leonardo to do various art projects, and while this was lucrative, Leonardo grew weary of the political games and **posturing** and slipped away to Milan. It was here that he would paint one of his most famous works on the wall of a convent: *The Last Supper*. This painting was unlike anything that had ever been done before because Leonardo painted a background with a perspective that was so well done it put you right in the scene at the table with the disciples! He spent years on this painting, working on it in fits and bursts between hanging out in the stables with his horses. When war descended Leonardo **pivoted** almost effortlessly from painter to inventor, creating military barricades to defend the city of Florence. Later he bounced around from chemistry—developing a new kind of varnish—to botany and even to human anatomy! In his final years, he became a close friend of King Francis I of France. Believed to have suffered from a stroke, Leonardo died at the age of 67 with many of his works fading into obscurity. His contemporaries classified him as a failure—a starter rather than a finisher who never gave his full attention to any one thing. Some believe that Leonardo himself regretted his lack of focus on one area, though those quotes are more speculation than fact. What do you think? Should he have honed in on his art?

SELF PORTRAIT BY LEONARDO DA VINCI

DID YOU KNOW? Leonardo da Vinci filled notebooks with sketches, designs, and inventions. He often wrote in code that only he could understand and would make notes from right to left (instead of left to right) so his work could only be read by using a mirror. If he was jotting down something for someone else, though, he could change his writing so the other person could understand it. Can you imagine writing in two different ways with ease? Looking at his work, many believe that he was actually dyslexic, a trait that gave him a brilliant mind that saw things in a unique and distinct way. Do you have any sort of learning challenges that make you different from others? These challenges might make reading and writing more difficult, but what if the very things that God put inside of you were meant to help you break the mold and see things in a new way? Who knows, maybe you'll be the next "Renaissance" man or woman!

NOTEBOOKING/LAPBOOK Alert

Find and label France (and/or Milan) on the map in your notebook or the back of your lapbook.

NOTABLE ART

Leonardo da Vinci may not have produced *as much* art as some of the artists who settled into their roles as a sort of "career," but what he brought to the table was no less profound. Let's take a look at his two most famous pieces, where they are found, and some of the things you should know about them.

The *Mona Lisa* is not only the most famous painting of the Renaissance, it is possibly the most famous piece of art all throughout history. Painted while Leonardo was still in Florence, it was a commissioned portrait of a nobleman's wife. First and foremost, the piece is unique because of how the subject is portrayed. Instead of being demure and subservient, the woman is making direct eye contact. She is also smiling, which was rare for the time period as most people were depicted with more solemn expressions. Instead of showing her whole body, Leonardo only focused on the upper portion, drawing attention away from her dress and toward her face. Painted using oil on wood, it stands today at the Louvre in France, where viewers are permitted 30 seconds to meet the mysterious woman's gaze before they are ushered out.

LEONARDO DA VINCI'S *MONA LISA* DISPLAYED AT THE LOUVRE MUSEUM IN PARIS, FRANCE

LEONARDO DA VINCI'S *THE LAST SUPPER* MURAL AT THE CONVENT OF SANTA MARIA DELLE GRAZIE IN MILAN, ITALY.

The *Last Supper* is a fresco, which is a painting made on the plaster of a wall or ceiling. Because plaster dries quickly, this technique was very difficult and required great skill, as there wasn't room for error. Leonardo, however, developed a technique that allowed him to work slowly on dried plaster. This meant that he could come back to it later. Sometimes he would stare at his work for hours or take long breaks, coming back with a fresh set of eyes. This painting is not one that can be transported in a frame. It is affixed in the convent it was originally painted in, requiring that the building be carefully protected and maintained to ensure that the work of art is not destroyed. Close-ups of the scene of Jesus and His disciples are powerful, but there is nothing like standing in the room and seeing how it all fits together. Eventually a doorway was cut into the wall under the painting, making the perspective of the painting seem almost like you are looking down the hallway.

NOTEBOOKING/LAPBOOK *Alert*

Add both of Leonardo da Vinci's paintings to your notebooking page and/or the museum in your lapbook and record what you like or don't like about them.

THE CHILDREN'S PRAYER REVIVAL

In the same way that Leonardo stood out as different, in 1708 a group of children also broke the mold. Along the border of the Czech Republic and Poland, there was a push to reestablish Catholicism as the main religion, and so persecution of evangelical Christians was a big problem. Evangelical churches and even Bibles were outlawed. Over 1,200 churches were shut down, pastors were exiled, and Protestant schools were closed, forcing students to go to Catholic ones instead. It was a dangerous time to disagree, and standing up for your beliefs had huge consequences. In the midst of this darkness however, God was moving. Families began to meet in secret outside the church in small gatherings where they were free to worship and pray. And it was a group of these children—all between 4 and 14 years old—who decided to do something radical. At the end of December 1707, they started holding prayer meetings in the hills. They decided to meet rain or shine three times a day: around 7:00 a.m., noon, and 4:00 p.m.—and at each service, the Holy Spirit met the group in power. Those who came were so touched that they would sometimes stay for 3–5 hours, and they counted the minutes until they could go back to pray again.

Kids from all over started to attend—hundreds of them! And in less than a week, five different regions were experiencing the same thing. No one had shared what was happening, yet somehow the same model was being followed in each of these areas. The children would gather in two circles—the boys in the middle and the girls in a larger circle around them. They would worship, sing hymns, and pray, kneeling and lying prostrate (or flat on the ground) before the Lord. They asked that they would be able to understand God's word, that their churches would be given back to them, that the Holy Spirit would send revival, and that they would be used by God. It didn't take long for the parents to notice that something was going on, and many began to attend to see what it was all about. Anyone who went was deeply touched by God's tangible presence, but not everyone was pleased. The Catholic leaders were not happy that this movement was happening outside of the church—where it was not in their control. They warned the parents to shut the meetings down, told their own children to stay away, and threatened to punish to the full extent of the law those who disobeyed. Naturally these parents were deeply concerned. One father tried to lock his children in their rooms so they would not go, but they simply threatened to jump out the windows, giving him no choice but to open the doors. Even Catholic children were drawn to the meetings as if their spirits knew that this revival was for *them*. The kids seemed completely unperturbed by the threats of their parents and the authorities. At one point officials even shot blank ammunition (producing a loud flash and bang but with no bullet) at the children to scare them, but the kids didn't even seem to flinch. Many signs and wonders followed. Their prayer books began to glow so they could read them even at night; doves were said to fly all around them as they prayed; and they experienced dreams and visions. These gatherings would trigger an incredible revival with more than 40,000 people participating each week. The children had done what their parents did not. They had broken through the layers of politics and religion and started a movement that could not be stopped. What could your prayers do?

DID YOU KNOW?

It's important to remember that no one is perfect. Some of the children who were a part of the revival were known to throw rocks at people who tried to stop them from praying. They weren't big fans of their parents getting involved or taking over either—they found that the adults' prayers were too short. One thing was for certain—the revival may not have lasted, but its effect did. Afterward the children who had been troublemakers or bullies were more mature and even became leaders among their peers. Those who had avoided school or viewed it as a chore began to take it more seriously. It was the true mark of revival—they had been transformed by the power of His Spirit, and the fruit was evident in their lives in an undeniable way.

VOCABULARY

EARLY READER
pivot: *to go in a different direction*
acclaim: *attention*

EARLY ELEMENTARY
acclaim: *attention*
replicate: *to make a copy of something*

UPPER ELEMENTARY
replicate: *to make a copy of something*
insatiable: *unable to be satisfied*

MIDDLE SCHOOL
insatiable: *unable to be satisfied*
piqued: *awakened; stirred*

HIGH SCHOOL
piqued: *awakened; stirred*
posturing: *behaving in a way that is not your true self in an effort to mislead someone*

HANDS-ON *Activity*

Try writing your name backwards like how Leonardo wrote and see if you can read it in a mirror. Can you design a secret code using different symbols? If you want to, develop one, and then take turns trying to decipher one another's work!

Renaissance and Revival

LESSON 6: MICHELANGELO

Your education of this time period would not be complete without a look at the renowned Michelangelo (no, not the Ninja Turtle). Named after the archangel Michael, this famous artist was born in 1475 to a well-off family in Italy. When he was still a baby, his family moved to Florence, but Michelangelo's time there would be brief. His mother died when he was six years old, and after her death he spent some time in the country with his wet nurse's family, who worked with stone. Here he was given his first hammer and chisel, and he began to discover a love for sculpting. When he got older, he was sent back to Florence to attend school. By this time it was considered the High Renaissance, and Florence was almost like a university town. It attracted artists and scholars from all over the world to study, practice, and even find work. Perhaps the passion was contagious because it didn't take long for Michelangelo to be swept up in it. In his early teens, he would go to churches and copy the art that he saw. Other artists would encourage him—and maybe even give him tips along the way. His father, on the other hand, did his best to **dissuade** Michelangelo from the arts. Some say that it was because being an artist was seen as a career below his station, but that didn't seem to bother the young lad at all; he continued to paint and sketch every chance he got. Eventually his father allowed him to **apprentice** under a painter named Ghirlandaio (*geer-lahn-deye-oh*). He was supposed to stay with the master for three years, but Michelangelo was a gifted **pupil**, and his skill was undeniable. When Lorenzo de' Medici asked Ghirlandaio to recommend some of his rising stars, Michelangelo's name came up, and it was only one year later that he—in his early teens—became a paid artist in his own right and was a student no longer.

MICHELANGELO PORTRAIT BY DANIELE DA VOLTERRA, C. 1545

TEACHER'S GUIDE LESSON 6   MICHELANGELO

The rise and fall of players in the game of life is not without its spectators, and Michelangelo's bold confidence, natural skill, and likely the attention he was receiving made him a target among his peers. He got into many disagreements—one of which resulted in him being punched in the face, breaking his nose. When Michelangelo was 21, a sponsor came to him with a proposition: Could he sculpt something that looked like an ancient artifact? He had plans to bury the piece and to sell it to an art dealer for a handsome profit. Michelangelo agreed to the challenge, creating his first **forgery**. The deal was placed, but it didn't take long for the buyer to realize that he had been deceived. Instead of getting angry, however, he seized the opportunity in front of him. Reaching out to Lorenzo, the man asked for the name of the artist so he could offer him a job in Rome. In an ironic twist, the very thing that could have ruined Michelangelo's budding career before it had even begun would be the thing that propelled him forward. Only a few years later, he would complete his 17-foot (about 5 m) statue of David, cementing himself as one of the leading artists of his time. He would go on to paint some of the most famous frescoes in the Sistine Chapel and to sculpt the *Pietà*, a statue of the Virgin Mary holding Jesus after his death. He even dabbled in architecture, designing and overseeing the construction of the dome over St. Peter's Basilica. Working until the day he died, Michelangelo left an unmistakable mark on the world both during the Renaissance and beyond. Where did it all start? With a chisel and hammer when he was six? Or maybe when he went to church and observed the colorful frescoes? One thing is for certain—the interests that you have today could just be passing curiosities, or they could be the very things that God has fashioned you for. What an adventure awaits!

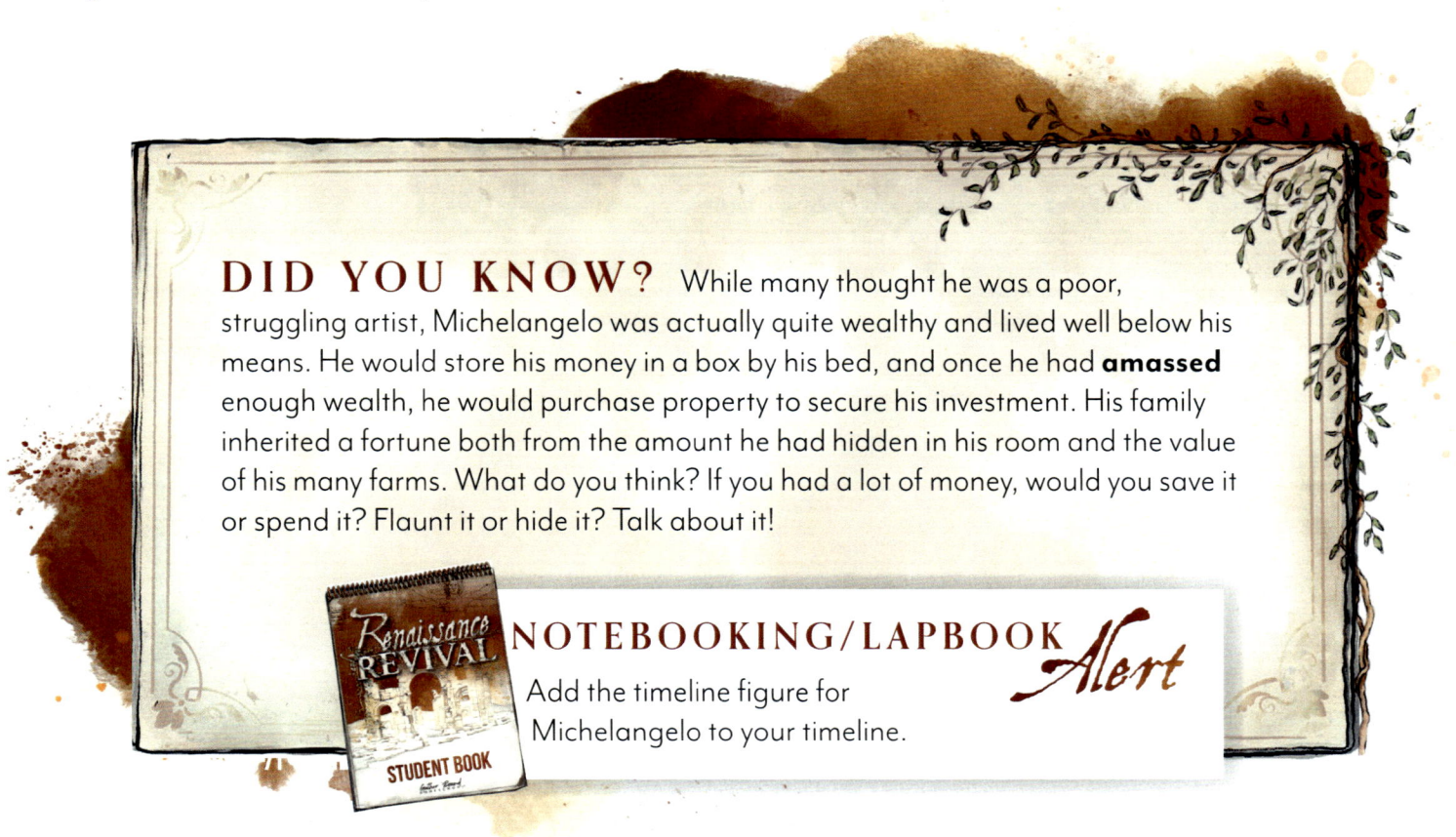

> "The greater danger for most of us lies not in setting our aim too high and falling short; but in setting our aim too low, and achieving our mark."[5]
> —attributed to Michelangelo

DID YOU KNOW? While many thought he was a poor, struggling artist, Michelangelo was actually quite wealthy and lived well below his means. He would store his money in a box by his bed, and once he had **amassed** enough wealth, he would purchase property to secure his investment. His family inherited a fortune both from the amount he had hidden in his room and the value of his many farms. What do you think? If you had a lot of money, would you save it or spend it? Flaunt it or hide it? Talk about it!

NOTEBOOKING/LAPBOOK *Alert*

Add the timeline figure for Michelangelo to your timeline.

MICHELANGELO'S MASTERPIECE: *THE CREATION OF ADAM* IN THE SISTINE CHAPEL, VATICAN MUSEUM IN ROME ITALY.

NOTABLE ART

One of the most recognizable works that Michelangelo created was his *David* statue, which the artist made when he was in his mid-twenties. This figure is *huge*, about as tall as an adult giraffe. It towers above its viewers and is very, very naked. Unlike Donatello's *David*, Michelangelo's sculpture was depicted as older—more like a man than a boy. He holds a sling on his shoulder and appears to be looking at a slightly different point with each eye, which many believe was an intentional imperfection on Michelangelo's behalf. This work had no name etched into it, but everyone knew who had crafted it. Today there are 30 **replicas** of the statue that have been made for display around the world. Perhaps the most incredible thing about the original creation is that it had been made from a single slab of marble, which had been thrown away because it was considered unusable due to its imperfections. What had been garbage to one person was recycled and used to create a masterpiece by another. What an amazing example of the famous quote, "When life gives you lemons, make lemonade."

Michelangelo's favorite art form was sculpting, and while he spent the majority of his career working with rock, a commission by the pope would trigger his very first fresco. The story goes that when the pope asked him to paint the ceiling of the Sistine Chapel, Michelangelo initially refused. There were plenty of other artists who specialized in this field, and the young artist preferred working with his chisel and hammer. But the pope was quite insistent, and so Michelangelo went to see what might be done. Originally commissioned to paint a scene depicting the 12 apostles, he ended up painting over 300 figures in many different scenes, including his most famous: *The Creation of Adam*. You might be familiar with the hand of God touching the hand of man, as this is commonly used as a symbol of the Renaissance and art in general. Painting that high up required scaffolding to be built, as well as a whole lot of neck craning. Some believe that Michelangelo painted some of the ceiling while lying on his back, but most records show that he painted it standing up with his arms above his head. However he did it, it would have been a long and uncomfortable four years. Many say that Michelangelo had never even painted a fresco before and had to be shown the basic techniques before he began. He might have been a master artist, but he was largely unqualified for a job of this magnitude. Nevertheless he took the challenge head-on and painted one of the most famous works of art that remains to this day.

MICHELANGELO'S *DAV*

TEACHER'S GUIDE LESSON 6

REVIVAL OF GOD'S WORD

Off the coast of Scotland on the island of Lewis, schools had been built that were designed to teach students to read and write through one textbook: the Bible. After the Bible was translated to Gaelic, the schools also allowed students to read it for themselves rather than having to go to church and listen to it in Latin, a language they didn't know or understand. Up until then there had been no books written in Gaelic, so no one in the villages was able to read or write. Unlike a dry, boring textbook, however, God's word is alive and powerful, and it didn't take long for His Spirit to move over the people. The island of Lewis revival all started with one little girl who was so struck by what she was reading that she came home and read it aloud to her sick mother. She recounted the story of Jesus' death, and her mother was so touched that she started crying. Concerned, the girl ran to the neighbor's house, convinced that her mother was in pain or that her sickness was getting worse. But her mother was not worse, only convicted of her sin. When the neighbor realized what was happening, she asked the girl to read the story to her too. The fact that Jesus would die for *her* impacted the neighbor in the same way, and now both women were overcome by their need for a Savior. By the time her father came home from work, the girl knew that the words she was reading were powerful, and so she shared what had happened. Her dad asked her to tell the story to him, and he was affected in the same way as the women. Because the people were unable to read, the little girl traveled from village to village reading the story of Jesus' death and resurrection, spreading the gospel message until a great number had turned to Christ.

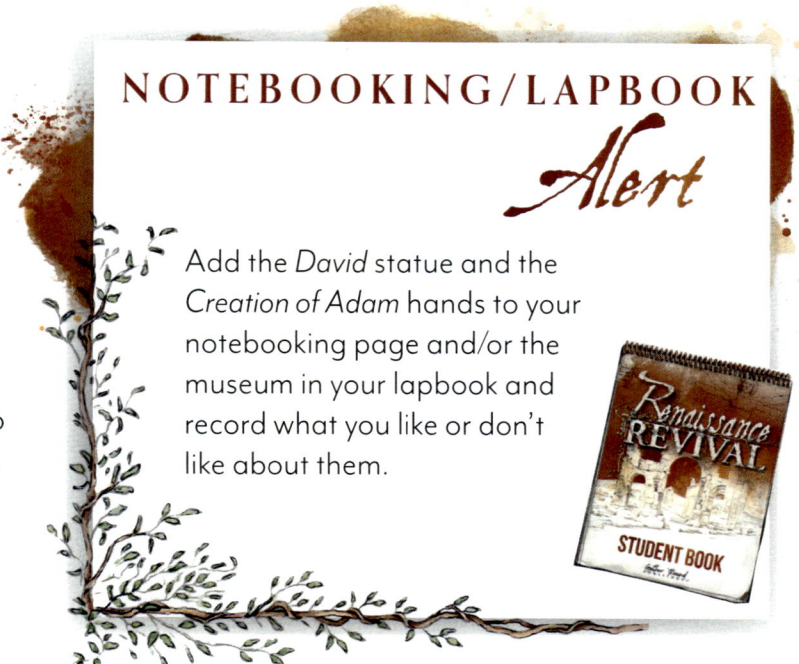

> **NOTEBOOKING/LAPBOOK *Alert***
>
> Add the *David* statue and the *Creation of Adam* hands to your notebooking page and/or the museum in your lapbook and record what you like or don't like about them.

Meanwhile the teachers at the schools also started holding services, but not everyone was happy about it. The original intention of the schools was to teach reading and writing, and the society that started them (as well as many local churches) was upset. It wanted to keep school and church separate, but those who spoke up were unable (and unwilling) to keep silent. One man in particular, John Macleod, ended up being fired from his job, yet he continued to preach out in the open, drawing huge crowds. Another was a young student who was only 14 years old. He was so affected by God's word that when he heard he could buy a Bible of his own, he traveled 20 miles on foot to purchase one. When he arrived in the town, he discovered that he didn't have enough money and had to walk another 20 miles back home to earn more before going back again. When he finally got his prize, he conducted public readings of God's word and became a teacher himself. Meetings were conducted all over the island in schools and outside services. The local ministers were jealous of the response that these untrained speakers were getting, and they tried to discredit the revival by saying that it was emotionalism—that people would shake and were mentally unstable. But the movement continued to spread. Eventually an Evangelical minister arrived and realized that while many people were convicted of their sin, they also needed to be discipled to know what a Christian walk looked like. He canceled communion, saying that no one was worthy to partake of it, and spent the next three years teaching the deeper elements of Christian living—such as holiness and even what communion meant. By the end of the revival, no village had been untouched. Thousands would gather for the services, undone with their own sin or interceding for others to be saved. The entire island had been radically changed—not through one great speaker, but through the power of God's word.

TEACHER'S GUIDE LESSON 6 — MICHELANGELO

HANDS-ON *Activity*

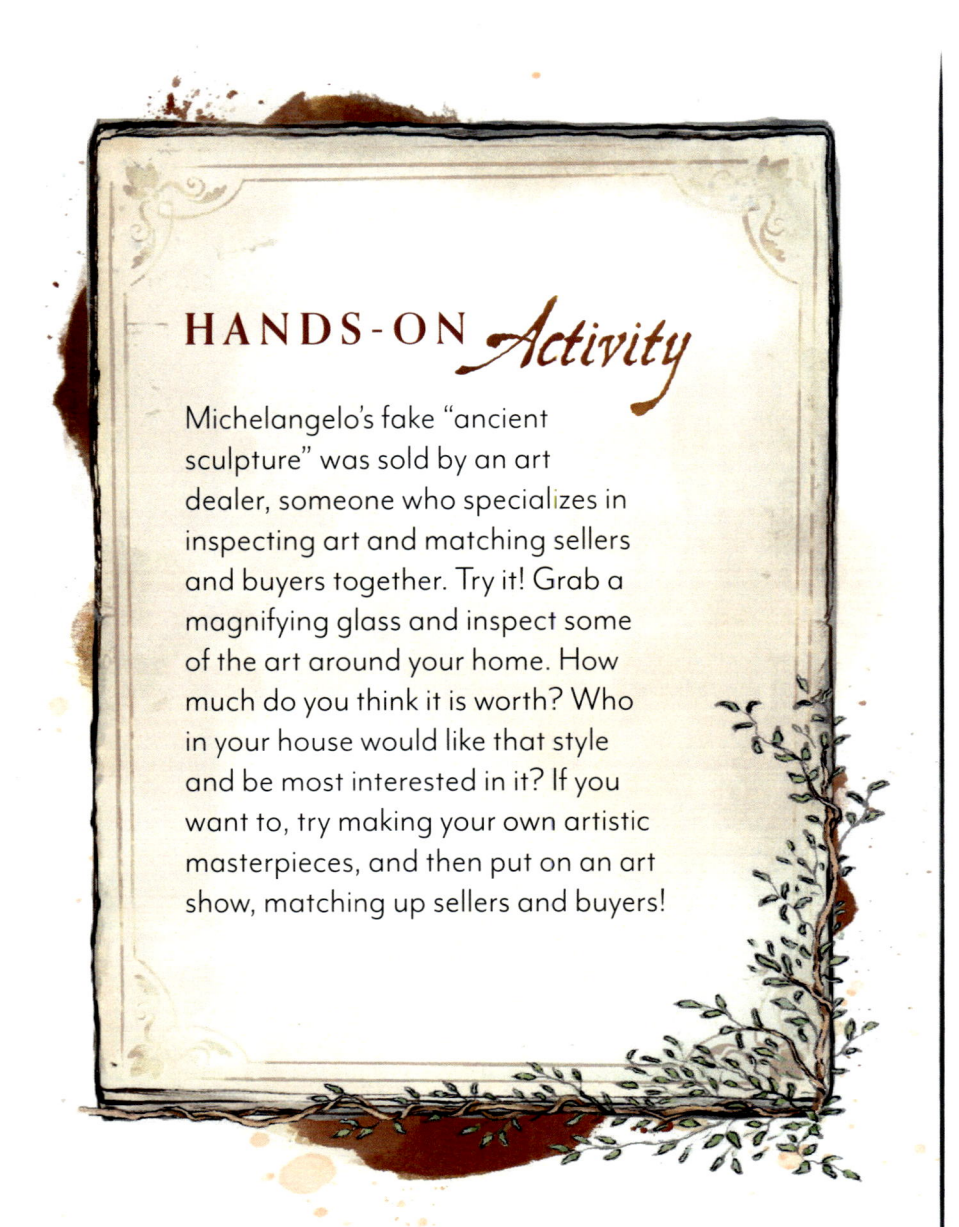

Michelangelo's fake "ancient sculpture" was sold by an art dealer, someone who specializes in inspecting art and matching sellers and buyers together. Try it! Grab a magnifying glass and inspect some of the art around your home. How much do you think it is worth? Who in your house would like that style and be most interested in it? If you want to, try making your own artistic masterpieces, and then put on an art show, matching up sellers and buyers!

VOCABULARY

EARLY READER
replica: *an exact copy*
pupil: *a student*

EARLY ELEMENTARY
pupil: *a student*
forgery: *something that is made to fool others into believing that it is the real thing*

UPPER ELEMENTARY
forgery: *something that is made to fool others into believing that it is the real thing*
apprentice: *someone who is learning a job by experience*

MIDDLE SCHOOL
apprentice: *someone who is learning a job by experience*
dissuade: *to convince someone not to do something*

HIGH SCHOOL
dissuade: *to convince someone not to do something*
amass: *to collect*

Renaissance and Revival

LESSON 7: RAPHAEL

There's no question: the Renaissance is inexplicably linked with art. In fact sometimes people get confused and attribute a lot more famous artists to this age than they should. But art is actually organized into different periods based on shared similarities—almost like how people go through the stages of being an infant, child, adolescent, and adult. Renaissance art was marked by similar feel and the use of similar techniques, but like watercolor on a wet canvas, art styles would continue to change and flow—from baroque to impressionism to surrealism to expressionism and more! Nowadays we get to build on the foundation started by all of the artists from these different periods. We can **dabble** in more classic art forms like those from the Renaissance or modern art like **abstract** pieces created with paint streaks, splatters, and drips. In the same way that there are no real fashion rules in the 21st century, there are no unifying art styles that mark this age. We are a product of the many who have gone before us, and we get to continue exploring the breakthroughs of the creators of yesterday. Let's take a closer look at one master artist whose name would go down in history as one of the greats.

MEET RAPHAEL

You know you're famous when nearly the whole world knows you by your first name—which is ironic because Raphael's real name was actually Raffaello Sanzio da Urbino. He was born in 1483 to a painter who provided him with his early training. His mother died when Raphael was only nine years old, and his father passed away shortly after that, leaving him an orphan. Raphael worked as an apprentice at the young age of eight, and by the time of his father's death, he had inherited his own studio. Unlike his contemporary Michelangelo, Raphael finished his apprenticeship, graduating when he was about 17 years old. By that time he had earned **recognition** as a master in his own right and had a well-developed skill set in multiple different art forms, styles, and techniques. Ready to build a name for himself, he took on his first commission—an oil painting. Having made his mark, he continued to rise in the art world both in **esteem** and skill. He had a unique ability of taking the styles of other artists and tweaking them to make them his own, leaving fingerprints of other influences in his work. You might have heard the saying, "**Imitation** is the best form of flattery," but other masters of the time such as Michelangelo and Leonardo were not convinced.

RAPHAEL

TEACHER'S GUIDE LESSON 7   39   **RAPHAEL**

With time and experience, Raphael started standing out, and it wasn't long before the pope invited him to Rome to work on more serious projects. Where Michelangelo's passion and strength were in sculpting, Raphael's was in painting. He gained the nickname Prince of Painters and worked on the pope's own quarters. He was known to start projects, sketching out his visions and plans, but then leave the rest of the work for his assistants to finish. With his eye for beauty, it wasn't long before Raphael was given architectural commissions to design chapels and churches. He even drew out plans for tapestries that would hang in the Sistine Chapel. He was one of the first artists to work with a printmaker to create prints of his works—which could be mass-produced and sold to many more people. In fact there were some pieces that he created specifically in order to be made into prints. To do this etchings were made that could be painted and then pressed onto paper. The copies were definitely different from the original works of art, mainly because they were mirrored (or facing the other way), but they began to open the door for more people to profit as artists—and for more people to own and appreciate art too. Raphael succeeded in carving out his place in history, and aspiring artists from all over flocked to train under him. As famous as he was in life, however, he was much more popular after his death. His works became more valuable, and his mastery was studied and appreciated around the world.

NOTEBOOKING/LAPBOOK *Alert*

Add the figure for Raphael to your timeline.

NOTABLE ART

This painting, which used oil on a wooden canvas, was made for a cardinal (who would later become the pope). He loved it so much that he kept it in his home for a time before eventually donating it to a church. The artwork was unique not just in style and **composition** but in the story that it told as well. It depicts multiple, different stories in one scene. Do you remember when Jesus took Peter, James, and John up to a mountain in Matthew 17? While they were there, the three disciples saw the face of Jesus transfigure, or change—His face shone, and His clothing became white. Moses and Elijah appeared and talked to Him as well. When God spoke the three disciples were terrified and fell to the ground. The moment would be forever recorded as the *Transfiguration*. The bottom half of the painting shows what happened next. A boy, who the disciples had been unable to free from his possession, was brought to Jesus. Jesus cast out the demons that the men could not. Raphael connected these two stories in his depiction, showing Jesus casting out the demon at the Transfiguration as a contrast to the attempts of man on the bottom. Later the painting was copied into prints so other artists could study it no matter where they were.

THE TRANSFIGURATION BY RAPHAEL, 1520

NOTEBOOKING/LAPBOOK *Alert*

Add *The Transfiguration* to your notebooking page and/or the museum in your lapbook and record either what you like or don't like about it.

THE SECOND GREAT AWAKENING

In the same way that the Renaissance spread like ripples in the water, the movement of God was unstoppable. For so long, religion had been impersonal and full of tradition rather than passion. Many people viewed God as distant and cold. They saw the church as being all about judgment and punishment—all rules and condemnation. As people encountered God for themselves, they saw their sin, yes, but they were also struck by His love and mercy for them. Faith became personal for a few, and their intimacy with God spurred many more to find Him for themselves. "Oh taste and see that the Lord is good"—Psalm 34:8a. Once they had tasted, they could not go back to the way things were. From one end of the Atlantic to the other, the renewal spread to America—a relatively new nation that was turning its back on God. Prior to the awakening, churches were closing their doors, and pastors were leaving their posts . . . people just weren't going to church anymore. From the biblical foundations that the country was built upon, it might have felt that things had slid too far—maybe the situation felt hopeless and unfixable. But we serve a God who can make all things new . . . and He had an outpouring in store that would shake the nation.

CAMP MEETING, BY HUGH BRIDPORT, CIRCA 1829

The Second Great Awakening was not a singular revival but rather a series of them that were passed on like a torch—lighting one region on fire and then the next. It all began in 1790 and continued on for over 40 years. These revivals were spread by ordinary people who were burdened for the lost. In Kentucky, things looked especially bleak, and one pastor was moved to gather with his people to pray. He advertised a joint communion service in Red River, and thousands came to it. The Holy Spirit showed up in power, and those who had gathered were deeply convicted of their sin. One pastor who was present took this revival fire to his hometown in Cane Ridge, advertising an open service. Over 20,000 people arrived, coming in wagons from all over the area. Various pastors from all backgrounds and denominations took up position among the crowd and started preaching. It was said that the children were not only deeply struck but also became powerful ministers in the revival—encouraging others and speaking with wisdom and authority far beyond their years. The revival spread from Kentucky outward to Ohio, Tennessee, and the Carolinas. The match had been struck!

TEACHER'S GUIDE LESSON 7

RAPHAEL

CHARLES G. FINNEY

If you've ever had a campfire, you know that flames must be fed and stoked so they keep burning. If you do not tend to them and fuel them, they will go out. In some places this is what seemed to start happening with the revival. One area in upstate New York became known as the Burned-over District because everyone there had been saved, and there was no new conviction of sin or salvation needed! It was from this well that a man named Charles Finney would emerge. He was a lawyer who encountered God in a very powerful way in 1821. After seeing a vision of Jesus face-to-face, he looked inside himself and discovered that his fire had gone out. As he sat down, he was filled with the power and fire of the Holy Spirit, and from then on nothing was the same. He walked away from his career and began preaching. At one meeting he found a man named Daniel Nash who was looking around the room, his lips moving in prayer. The two decided to band together, and they became an incredible team—Charles Finney might have been the mouth and face of the revivals that were going on, but Father Nash (as he was referred to) was behind the scenes interceding for every meeting. Charles would send Father Nash ahead of him to pray and to prepare a place for the upcoming gathering. The prayer warrior would find a little room, an alcove outside, or some quiet space and pray with everything he had. He was known to lie flat on the ground, break out in a cold sweat from his fervent prayer, and even groan where other people could hear him. He usually didn't go to the meetings, choosing instead to hide away in a room and pray. For seven years the two worked together, tirelessly contending for the salvation of lost souls. When Father Nash died, Charles stepped down from his traveling ministry and took a job at a church as its pastor. Many say that he felt the loss of power because he had lost his prayer partner. Today Charles Finney is the name that is remembered in many regions, with Father Nash being an almost forgotten figure who many never even knew existed. Yet one man's prayers were like the fuel on the fire—stoking the flames so just one more person would be saved. A great awakening indeed.

VOCABULARY

EARLY READER
dabble: *to take part in something in a small, unofficial way*
abstract: *having no specific shape or style*

EARLY ELEMENTARY
abstract: *having no specific shape or style*
imitation: *copying what others do and say*

UPPER ELEMENTARY
imitation: *copying what others do and say*
recognition: *attention given for one's accomplishments*

MIDDLE SCHOOL
recognition: *attention given for one's accomplishments*
composition: *the arrangement of subject(s) in a piece of art*

HIGH SCHOOL
composition: *the arrangement of subject(s) in a piece of art*
esteem: *respect and great admiration*

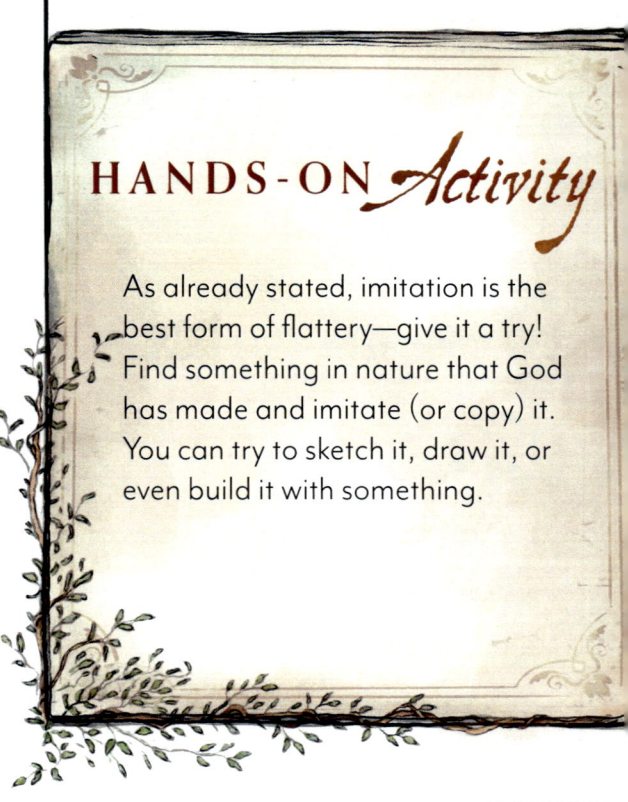

HANDS-ON *Activity*

As already stated, imitation is the best form of flattery—give it a try! Find something in nature that God has made and imitate (or copy) it. You can try to sketch it, draw it, or even build it with something.

TEACHER'S GUIDE LESSON 7   RAPHAEL

Renaissance and Revival

LESSON 8: HENRY VIII

Do you remember how the Renaissance started in Italy and then spread out from there? Like a river bursting through a dam, the Renaissance roared toward France, England, Germany, and beyond. At the same time, the House of Tudor (a line of monarchs who would rule in England) was established. Like it or not, things were changing. But people did have a bit of help from one particular king: Henry VIII. Unlike Lorenzo or Cosimo de' Medici—whose passions for art, literature, and architecture propelled the Renaissance forward—Henry VIII pushed the period forward almost by accident. His own selfish ambitions had very real consequences for the nation as a whole, and he would serve as an **instigator** that would inflame the battle between Protestants and Catholics. From one perspective, you might say that things went from bad to worse. Yet when you look at the bigger picture, it is easy to see how God used the **folly** of man to bring about very real revival and change in the lives of individuals in England and beyond. Let's take a closer look at the fascinating story of King Henry VIII to see how his actions would start a religious war that would change everything.

BEFORE THE BREAK

Henry was born into royalty in 1491. His father (also named Henry) was the king of England, and generally speaking, a good one. Henry VIII had three siblings, including one brother named Arthur. All of them were married off in strategic connections that formed alliances and secured allies. Arthur was wed to a Spanish princess, Catherine of Aragon, but died only a short time later, leaving Henry as heir to the throne. When his father died, Henry was encouraged to take his brother's widow as his own wife, and he agreed to do it, becoming both a husband and king when he was only 17 years old. Catherine was older than her young groom, and for a while, the two had a happy marriage—though that would not last. During this time in history, women were expected to do one thing: have babies. In particular they had a responsibility to produce a male heir who could carry on the family name, and Catherine failed to do this. Her tragic story is one of loss and grief and yet deep, unwavering devotion to the Catholic faith. She only produced one healthy girl, Mary, losing six others over the years to miscarriage, stillbirth, and illness. After nearly 18 years of marriage, Henry grew weary of Catherine. He blamed her for not having a son, and he set his eyes on someone younger: Catherine's lady-in-waiting, Anne Boleyn.

NOTEBOOKING/LAPBOOK Alert

Find and mark England on the map on your notebooking page or in your lapbook.

Like having a shiny new coin, Henry felt that Anne would fix things and make him happy, but what she saw was an opportunity to be queen. She encouraged the king's affections but determined that they would have to be married in order to be together. This issue would become known as "the King's great matter," as it took center stage in England. The Catholic church viewed divorce as a sin, so Henry's only hope was to get the pope to annul his marriage. To build his case, he used Leviticus 20:21, which states that anyone who marries his brother's wife will be childless. However, Henry had been married for 18 years and had one healthy child, so the pope refused to grant his request, enraging the king. Henry married Anne in secret and was excommunicated from the Catholic church. To fix the problem, he created his own church—the Church of England—and divorced Catherine, forcing her to leave. *Now* he would be happy, right? Wrong. Just like all shiny, new things that become old fast, Anne was no exception. Though she made a valiant effort to be loved by the people and to do what Catherine could not, Anne was also unable to produce a male heir. The English people had loved their regal and devout Queen Catherine, and they saw Anne as a **usurper**, no matter how hard she and Henry tried to convince them otherwise. After Anne gave birth to a daughter, Elizabeth, the king perhaps finally accepted that he might not have a son, and he passed the Act of Supremacy and Acts of Succession, declaring himself as the head of the church and Elizabeth as his rightful heir (rather than Mary). After only three years of marriage to Anne, Henry found another shiny new coin at the court—a lady-in-waiting named Jane Seymour. Not wanting to divorce another wife, he came up with charges against Anne and sentenced her to death.

AFTER HANS HOLBEIN THE YOUNGER - PORTRAIT OF HENRY VIII VIII, CIRCA 1537

AFTER THE SPLIT

At the same time as all of this drama was happening, the nation of England was in turmoil. With the invention of the printing press, reformers like William Tyndale and Martin Luther were rising up. Tyndale created an English translation of the Bible that was printed and shared, and Luther came up against some of the theology of the Catholic church. These two men would become key players in what would become known as the Protestant Reformation. And while you might think that Henry would have been supportive of this movement because of his own problems with the pope, he seemed to only encourage what served his own purposes. In fact he sent men to find Tyndale so he might be executed, and his version of the Bible was outlawed as heresy. So was the Church of England Protestant? Not really. The reality is, although Henry had left the Catholic church, he was still Catholic in his beliefs. This caused a lot of confusion for the English people. Henry's stance against the pope forced him to ease up on the Protestant movement, but he never fully supported it either. The Church of England became a **hybrid** of sorts—a blend between both Catholic and Protestant theology. And Henry? Well, he continued his great search for happiness after the death of Jane Seymour, beheading one more wife and divorcing another before he passed away and ultimately leaving a legacy of selfishness in his wake.

> **DID YOU KNOW?** Henry might have had selfish motivations, but the shaky ground that he created weakened the strong arm of the Catholic church, leaving room for the Protestant Reformation to grow and flourish. It added fuel to this renaissance of religion . . . and strengthened one of the greatest church splits in history.

NOTEBOOKING/LAPBOOK Alert
Add the figure for Henry VIII to your timeline.

NOTABLE LITERATURE
One of the king's greatest advisors was Sir Thomas More, a highly educated man who was deeply devoted to the Catholic church, his family, and his work. Originally trained as a lawyer, he ended up going into politics instead. His Catholic beliefs led him to openly stand against the Protestant Reformation, and he ordered for no less than six people to be executed for heresy. He would go on to write a book called *Utopia*, a short description of a fictional society where everything was shared equally among the people (kind of like how socialism works). When it came to "the King's great matter," Thomas stood staunchly with the pope, and it was this zeal that would eventually cost him his life. As a prominent member of society and close friend of the king, Thomas was given multiple opportunities to "change his tune," but he turned them down. He did not attend the king's marriage to Anne, and when it came to the Act of Supremacy, he stoically refused to sign it. The king had Thomas arrested for treason and executed him only four days later.

NOTABLE ARCHITECTURE
During this time, religion wasn't the only thing being reformed. Like in Italy the Renaissance was advancing art, culture, philosophy, science, math, and architecture in England as well. While King Henry VIII was on the throne, the King's College Chapel was completed, one of the most iconic buildings at Cambridge University that still stands today. It was started by Henry's great-grandfather, and its beautiful stained-glass windows were finished in the midst of all the turmoil of Henry VIII's reign. Because it took so long to finish, the chapel was built in the more Gothic style that marked the Middle Ages rather than the classical style of the Renaissance. But its beauty makes it a striking addition to England's architecture and story. Pull out your notebook/lapbook and complete the section about the chapel.

KING'S COLLEGE CHAPEL

HAWAIIAN REVIVAL

Have you ever heard of the Great Commission? Before Jesus rose into heaven after his resurrection, He told His apostles to "Go therefore and make disciples of all nations"—Matthew 28:19a. It's no surprise, then, that one of the results of the Second Great Awakening was an increase in mission work. Many who were touched by the power of God surrendered their lives to Him, not just in a spiritual sense but in a very real sense as well. People walked away from their jobs, security, and homes to spread the good news of great joy that they had heard. One such man was Titus Coan, who felt called to go to Hawaii (then known as the Sandwich Islands) in 1835. Titus was not the first missionary to travel to the islands, which were **notorious** for the pagan beliefs of their citizens. People worshiped the goddess Pele (of fire and volcanoes), and there was a priest and priestess who encouraged the locals to offer their children as sacrifices to appease the deity in order to keep the volcanoes away. Early missionaries worked to learn the language and customs of the people and to teach them about the grace and mercy of Jesus Christ . . . and it worked. The native people were open to this God who required nothing from them but faith and surrender. Some of them were moved to start praying for their people and to ask God to send revival. In fact even the children were known to weep and pray for God to move among the people. And it was into this **primed** environment that Titus Coan would find himself.

Titus did a number of tours, traveling throughout the villages and preaching multiple times a day to the region surrounding Hilo. The people were responsive, gathering in large numbers and crowding the man of God so there was barely time for him to eat or sleep. Even the priest and priestess of Pele came to listen, and they were so moved that they publicly confessed that they had been deceived by a false god and gave their lives to Jesus. No one could have imagined what would happen next: in 1837 a tsunami crashed into the island with no warning, devastating villages and claiming about 13 lives. But what the enemy surely meant for evil, God would use for His glory and for the good of the people in Hawaii. The locals were struck with the far-too-close reality of death, coming face-to-face with the fact that it could have been any of them who died in that wave. And as a direct result, the meetings grew exponentially. Titus' own town of Hilo grew from 1,000 people to 10,000, as new converts packed up and moved to be closer to the church there. A great revival swept through the services, marked by the same signs and wonders of so many before—with many people falling down under the power of the Holy Spirit and the conviction of their sin, weeping, and asking what they must do to be saved. The result was lasting change. Titus and the other missionaries discipled and worked with the new converts, teaching them the ways of the Lord. Armed with the gospel message, believers were sent out in groups of two (just like Jesus sent the disciples) to spread out and share God's word with all the people of the islands. Who would have imagined that a catastrophe could trigger a powerful revival? The prayers of the locals were answered, and God met the Hawaiian people, changing them forever.

HANDS-ON *Activity*

Have you ever thought that something new would make you happy, only to grow tired of it and want something else just a short time later? It is important to learn how to be content and thankful with what we have and to make sure that the things we want are wise and right, but this isn't easy—even for adults! As a family take some time to make a list of all the things you have and are thankful for. Then if you want, think about some of the things you've been asking for or that you want and pray about them. Is it the right time for them? Are they the right priority? Ask the Lord to help you to seek true, lasting joy in Him rather than in the fleeting happiness of things. You could even give something of yours away to someone who needs it and see which truly satisfies you . . . getting or giving.

VOCABULARY

EARLY READER
folly: *foolish behavior*
primed: *prepared*

EARLY ELEMENTARY
primed: *prepared*
hybrid: *a mixture of two or more things*

UPPER ELEMENTARY
hybrid: *a mixture of two or more things*
instigator: *a person who causes something to happen*

MIDDLE SCHOOL
instigator: *a person who causes something to happen*
notorious: *unfavorably known for something*

HIGH SCHOOL
notorious: *unfavorably known for something*
usurper: *a person who forcefully takes someone's place*

Renaissance and Revival

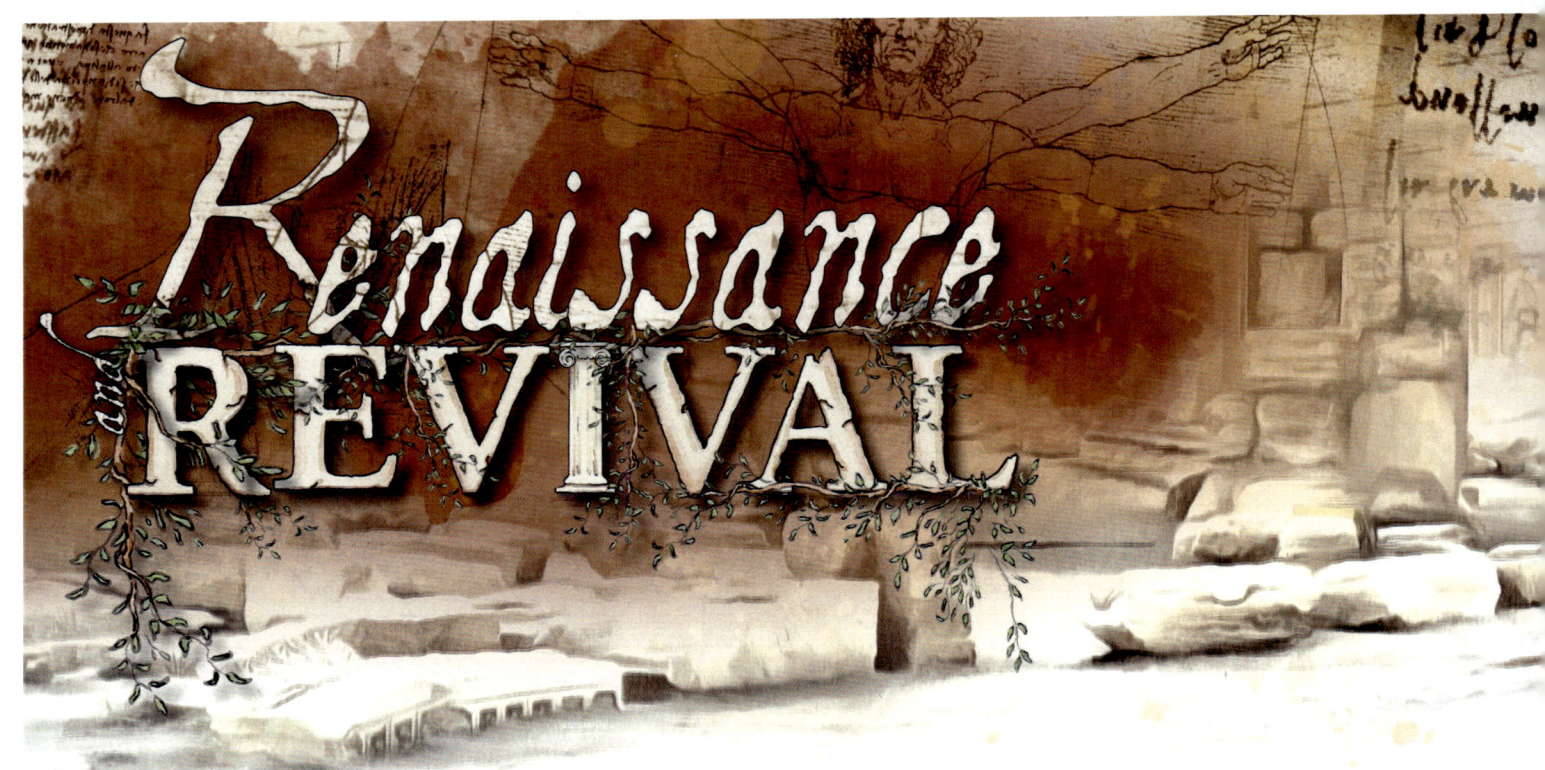

LESSON 9: DESIDERIUS ERASMUS

When most people think of the Protestant Reformation, Martin Luther is often the first name that comes to mind. Luther challenged the Catholic Church on a number of different points and began **advocating** for reform and change within it. But he was far from the only domino that would fall, leading to the split of the Protestant Church from the Catholic Church. Other men also rose up and questioned the status quo. One of these religious pioneers—Desiderius *(Deh-suh-deh-ree-uhs)* Erasmus—had a complicated relationship with Luther. The two men undeniably agreed about one thing: change was necessary. But they clashed over what that change should be and how it should happen. In fact they even wrote letters and published essays arguing with one another in an attempt to prove their points. These two men would continue an age-old debate about the free will of mankind and what that meant for salvation. Few people agree on this topic even today! But like it or not, Luther and Erasmus were key players in the religious reform that was taking place all around them.

EARLY LIFE

Erasmus was born in 1469 in the Netherlands, which made him older than Michelangelo, Raphael, and even Henry VIII. It's strange to think that he lived at the same time as many of the great men you have already learned about, and yet he ran in very different circles. His father was a priest, so he was educated early on and eventually sent to a Catholic school that specialized in preparing boys to be monks. He served as a monk for some time before becoming a priest and attending a school in Paris to learn more about theology. For the next 20 years, Erasmus would build a name for himself, not as an artist like some of the other men we've studied but rather as a scholar. After studying philosophy and ancient literature while **pondering** deeper questions about faith and religion, he began to write short works and teach throughout Europe. He was even invited to England to meet the young prince (at the time), Henry VIII, as well as Thomas More. Erasmus believed strongly in the power of education and the importance of studying original works rather than relying on other interpretations. This perspective even led him to translate a new version of the Bible from the original Greek text.

NOTEBOOKING/LAPBOOK Alert

Find and mark the Netherlands on the map on your notebooking page or in your lapbook.

TEACHER'S GUIDE LESSON 9 — DESIDERIUS ERASMUS

With the invention of the printing press, Erasmus was able to publish his works and grow his name. He became one of the leading minds in combining religion with the philosophy of humanism to show how it could all fit together. In fact many of his quotes are still referred to and used today. Erasmus loved the church but felt that it had grown **corrupt** and therefore needed to be cleansed and changed. And it was at this point in history that our story truly begins. During King Henry VIII's reign, Martin Luther and Erasmus would stand on two sides of the same coin, both believing that Christians needed to have personal relationships with God. Luther would publish a list of things that he saw as problems in the Roman Catholic Church. On some of these points, Erasmus would **vehemently** disagree. Luther saw himself as far more superior than Erasmus in logic, reasoning, and doctrine, while Erasmus felt that Luther was going to extremes by not leaving room for some of the mystery of God. Erasmus responded publicly to Luther's 95 points, debating them in the public forum of literature, and Luther retaliated with a written argument of his own. In their lifetimes the two men would not see eye to eye on many things. But their **discourse** would be like fuel on the fire of the Protestant Reformation, stoking the flames until they would become unstoppable.

DESIDERIUS ERASMUS

NOTEBOOKING/LAPBOOK Alert

Add the figure for Desiderius Erasmus to your timeline and complete the section to study some of his famous quotes!

DID YOU KNOW? The topics of free will and predestination cause *huge* debates in the church today. Two men also born around this same time period would expand on the debate between Erasmus and Luther. Their names were John Calvin and Jacobus Arminius—the fathers of Calvinism and Arminianism. Are we predestined and chosen to be saved? Do we have a choice in the matter? Can anyone truly be saved, or can only the few elect? Is salvation a gift that we choose to receive? What about the verse that states God is "not wishing that any should perish"?[6] All churches have an opinion on these matters, and it is important to wrestle through exactly what you believe with the Holy Spirit. Where does your family stand on these things? Why?

Though Erasmus was Catholic and a priest himself, his suggestion that the church was full of corruption and that it needed to change was considered a threat. He, like Luther, stood against the idea of selling indulgences and felt that a personal relationship with Jesus was the only way that a person could be saved. After his death his books—along with Luther's—were outlawed, and it even became illegal to own Erasmus' translation of the Bible. However, these prohibitions wouldn't last, and eventually his works would be removed from the list of books forbidden by the Catholic Church. Ironically though Luther and Erasmus disagreed on some major points, Luther would use Erasmus' Bible and methods to create a German Bible translation. People say that "hindsight is 20/20," and looking back, it is easy to see that Erasmus played a huge role in both the Northern Renaissance and the Protestant Reformation as a whole.

NOTABLE ART

Meanwhile over in Italy, the Italian Renaissance was still going strong, and new painters were rising up every day. One artist you haven't met yet is Titian, a painter in the early-1500s who was about as famous as Michelangelo. Titian was born in Venice around 1490, and his real name was actually Tiziano Vecelli. Like many of his contemporaries, he showed incredible promise from a young age, and by the time he was 10 or 12, he was immersed in the art world under a master painter. His skills grew, and he eventually became a painter in his own right, taking commissions from clients far beyond his hometown. He was so confident in his abilities that he was said to have worked with his fingers as much as his brushes, moving the paint to gain the desired effect he was going for. To say the least, many of Titian's paintings were "revealing" (or contained a lot of nudity), which fit with the times as artists sought to capture a more classical style. Titian was most famous for his use of color, and long after his death his paintings would go on to inspire other artists all over the world—including the renowned Rembrandt. Study the painting on the right and take a few minutes to just look at it. What stands out to you the most? Where does Titian use shadow and light to draw your eye? What do you think is happening in this painting? This work is titled *The Assumption of the Virgin* and shows Mary on a cloud being lifted up to heaven; many Catholics believe that instead of dying, Mary was "assumed" into heaven while she was still alive. This painting is 22 feet (about 7 m) tall and stands in a church in Venice to this day.

TITIAN'S *THE ASSUMPTION OF THE VIRGIN* AT BASILICA OF SANTA MARIA GLORIOSA DEI FRARI IN VENICE, ITALY

NOTEBOOKING/LAPBOOK *Alert*

Paste the painting onto your notebook page or inside your museum in the lapbook and write or discuss your thoughts about it.

TEACHER'S GUIDE LESSON 9   **DESIDERIUS ERASMUS**

CIVIL WAR REVIVALS

Throughout history disagreements have often gone far beyond words. Although Luther and Erasmus published arguments, essays, and letters debating each other, one disagreement in the United States would create a great divide that would eventually lead to war. The American Civil War was fought between the North and the South, also known as the Yankees (Unionists) and Rebels (Confederates). There was a line drawn in the sand, and people were forced to choose a side and fight in the most deadly war in American history. (Yes, it was even more deadly than World War I and II combined!) Yet it was here, amid the literal valley of the shadow of death, that the Holy Spirit moved in power as only He can do. Let's take a closer look . . .

In the early stages of war, soldiers were enticed to join the battle with promises of glory, fame, and adventure. Young boys left home with **naive** visions of grandeur, determined to prove themselves as men. As is often the case with peer pressure, the soldiers tried to fit in by drinking, smoking, brawling, cursing, and doing other such things that they thought might impress their buddies. When the fighting began, however, it didn't take long for these young men to be confronted with the idea of their own mortality. Conditions in the camps were often horrible, with many soldiers dying from sickness, infection, or simply starvation. One by one the men watched their friends die, and they were quickly sobered, missing home and the innocence they had inadvertently exchanged. The South was greatly outnumbered, and that reality carried with it a desperation that only an act of God could change—and so the people began to pray. Revival was first documented in the midst of Lee's army in Virginia, though it would spread rapidly. Where soldiers had once scoffed at attending services, they now amassed in great numbers, hungry for the hope that could be offered there. Temporary chapels and churches were built with haste, and chaplains came from near and far to minister to the desperate soldiers. They could not keep up with the demand for tracts. Thousands of people were saved—with many being baptized in the river overlooking enemy camps—and entire companies were changed. Each new battle or defeat would bring waves of repentance and salvation. Letters began pouring home from boys wanting their moms to know that they had found Jesus and that if they never made it home . . . there was still hope. Prayers for the South to be victorious were ultimately not answered—at least not in the way that people had imagined. Yet there was victory over darkness, and the true enemy was defeated for many people. Historians recorded many things about the American Civil War, which led to the making of television shows and movies depicting the brutal conflict. However, few retold the undeniable accounts of the great move of God and His incredible grace that accompanied and forever changed both sides of the battle lines. So we will tell the story . . . lest we forget that God is on the side of each and every soul, not wishing that any should perish.[7]

Only take care, and keep your soul diligently, lest you forget the things that your eyes have seen, and lest they depart from your heart all the days of your life. Make them known to your children and your children's children.
—Deuteronomy 4:9

HANDS-ON *Activity*

Test your vision! Having 20/20 vision means that you can see with clarity both far away and close up—and sometimes we can't see a situation clearly until we have moved through it. Print off an eye test chart (there's one on the resources page on the app) and pick a distance at which to test your own family's vision.

VOCABULARY

EARLY READER
ponder: *to think about something*
naive: *not having much experience or knowledge about something*

EARLY ELEMENTARY
naive: *not having much experience or knowledge about something*
corrupt: *dishonest*

UPPER ELEMENTARY
corrupt: *dishonest*
advocate: *to defend or support a cause*

MIDDLE SCHOOL
advocate: *to defend or support a cause*
discourse: *an exchange of ideas through conversation*

HIGH SCHOOL
discourse: *an exchange of ideas through conversation*
vehemently: *with strong emotions*

Renaissance and Revival

LESSON 10: MARTIN LUTHER

Martin Luther was born in 1483 in a small town in eastern Germany. His father was a miner who wanted a better life for his young son, so he sent Martin to school when the boy was about seven years old with hopes that he would become a **profitable** lawyer. Things were looking good for young Luther, who grew up on the the subjects of logic, rhetoric, Latin, and even philosophy. When he was 22 years old, however, a profound encounter would forever change the trajectory of his life. With his studies in law just begun, Luther decided to go home to visit his family, and on the way he was caught in a horrible thunderstorm. This wasn't a normal storm. It was violent and terrifying—Luther was certain that he would die. He found shelter in the cleft of a rock and while waiting made a **vow**, "Help me, Saint Anne, and I will become a monk."[8] If you aren't Catholic, this might seem like a strange prayer, but it was common at the time for people to pray to patron saints, who they believed would petition before the Lord on their behalf. St. Anne, believed to be the mother of the Virgin Mary, was also the patron saint of miners; Luther would have been familiar with St. Anne because of his father's job. When the storm finally passed, Martin felt that his prayer had been answered, and he was determined to uphold his promise. Upon returning home he sold all of his books and entered a monastery, devoting his life to God.

MARTIN LUTHER

THINK ABOUT IT

Hebrews 4:16 says, "Let us then with confidence draw near to the throne of grace, that we may receive mercy and find grace to help in time of need." There is no intermediary that needs to stand between us and God. Because of Jesus the veil was torn, and we ourselves can go into the Holy of Holies to meet the great I AM face-to-face in the secret places of our hearts. With the Holy Spirit to guide us, we do not rely on people to speak to God for us. Instead we can talk to God directly ourselves! It is important to note that the Catholic Church today *does* teach that believers can go to Jesus directly. But it also says that believers can **beseech** the saints to intercede on their behalf. This belief comes primarily from the *Apocrypha*, a group of books that are not in the Protestant Bible because they were not determined to be holy scriptures. How does your family feel about praying to saints?

NOTEBOOKING/LAPBOOK Alert

Pull out your timeline figures and place the cutout for Martin Luther in the correct spot to show how he fits into the story! Then mark Germany on the map to show where he was from.

For the next decade or so of his life, Luther would gain his doctorate of theology (much to the disappointment of his father) and spent his days **immersed** in his pursuit of God. He wrestled with his salvation, plagued with self-doubt and insecurity as he poured over the scriptures. Eventually he began teaching. And it was as he opened God's word to others that God's word was revealed to him. Luther was struck by the idea of justification through faith alone rather than through works. He felt that the stance of the Roman Catholic Church—particularly on indulgences—was wrong, and he could not stay silent. On October 31, 1517, in Wittenberg, Germany, Luther nailed his arguments onto the door of the church, which was no accident considering the next day was All Saints' Day and the building would be packed. Congregants would be forced to pass by his statement—which would become known as the 95 Theses—making it impossible to ignore. Though originally written in Latin, the document was quickly translated into German and mass-produced—making it all the way to the papacy in Rome. As you might imagine, the pope was not amused.

DID YOU KNOW?

Nowadays October 31 is most commonly known as Halloween, but it is also called Reformation Day in honor of the spark of the 95 Theses that triggered the Protestant Reformation.

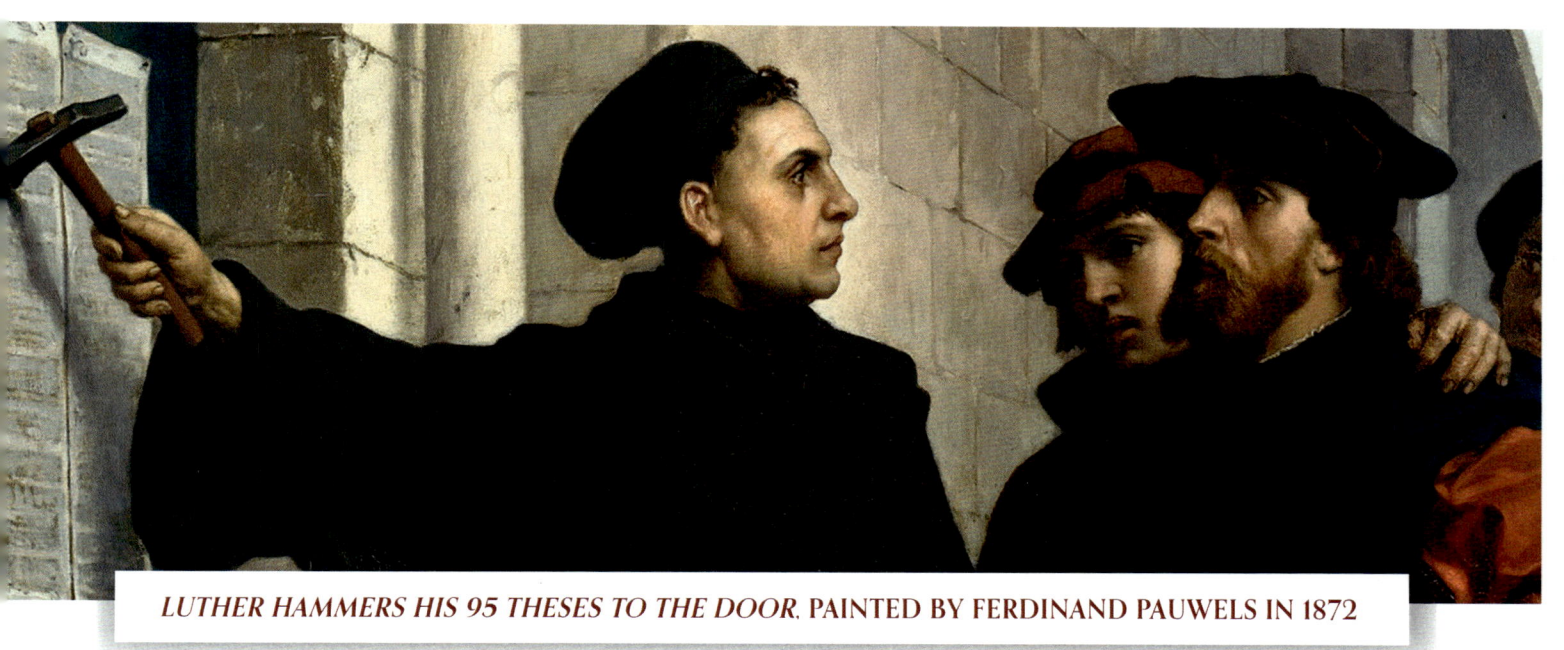

***LUTHER HAMMERS HIS 95 THESES TO THE DOOR.* PAINTED BY FERDINAND PAUWELS IN 1872**

This document was not originally intended to divide or break up the church. Rather, Luther wanted his statements to be argued and considered. What he found most **abhorrent** in the practice of indulgences was that priests were charging money in exchange for forgiveness, something that Luther felt was completely wrong. The 95 points built on one another and were more like statements that created an overall argument. Let's take a look at some of the things he said:

27. They preach only human doctrines who say that as soon as the money clinks into the money chest, the soul flies out of purgatory.

32. Those who believe that they can be certain of their salvation because they have indulgence letters will be eternally damned, together with their teachers.

36. Any truly repentant Christian has a right to full remission of penalty and guilt, even without indulgence letters.

45. Christians are to be taught that he who sees a needy man and passes him by, yet gives his money for indulgences, does not buy papal indulgences but God's wrath.

46. Christians are to be taught that, unless they have more than they need, they must reserve enough for their family needs and by no means squander it on indulgences.

54. Injury is done to the Word of God when, in the same sermon, an equal or larger amount of time is devoted to indulgences than to the Word.

56. The true treasures of the church, out of which the pope distributes indulgences, are not sufficiently discussed or known among the people of Christ.

65. Therefore the treasures of the gospel are nets with which one formerly fished for men of wealth.

86. Again, "Why does not the pope, whose wealth is today greater than the wealth of the richest Crassus, build this one basilica of St. Peter with his own money rather than with the money of poor believers?"[9]

Luther ultimately spoke of greed, corruption, and a passive reliance on the quick fix of paying money to absolve oneself from guilt rather than practicing true repentance. He saw some big problems that he wanted revealed and addressed. For a few years, his points were challenged and fiercely debated back and forth, but the pope quickly grew weary of the conflict as well as the significant damage it was causing to the overall unity of the church. In 1518 Luther was ordered to recant his positions—which he **doggedly** refused to do. When he received letters threatening excommunication, he publicly burned them, and the papacy eventually followed through with its threats in 1521. Luther became a wanted man, and his works were banned by the church, but that didn't stop him. He continued to write, speak, debate, and lecture—he even wrote a German translation of the Bible so people could read God's word for themselves. Those who followed his teachings (along with other reformers of the time) became known as *protesters*, which is where the term *Protestant Reformation* came from. The divide was greatly helped by Henry VIII, who also stood against the Roman Catholic Church (though for far different reasons), and the reformation continued to spread through different revivals all over the world.

DID YOU KNOW? As with all people, Luther made mistakes. The Bible says that "For now we see in a mirror dimly, but then face to face. Now I know in part; then I shall know fully, even as I have been fully known"—1 Corinthians 13:12. Like all of humanity, Luther did not have full revelation of who God was, and his beliefs were expounded on by others who would come after him. He believed that the Jewish religion's rejection of Jesus was intolerable, and he came strongly against Jewish people, even suggesting violence like burning their houses. The Lutheran Church became well established in Germany, and these antisemitic views unfortunately permeated the hearts and minds of many. In fact the Nazis would capitalize on these teachings, using them as an excuse of sorts for what would become known as the Holocaust. It is important to remember that all great men and women throughout history (or even those who inspire us today) are still people, and we must discern and follow God's word over the words of man—testing everything by His Spirit to receive what is good and lovely and pure and to reject what is not.

NOTEBOOKING/LAPBOOK *Alert*
Pull out your notebook and write, draw, or dictate (or put together the book) to show what you learned about Martin Luther.

THE WELSH REVIVAL

Wales had tasted revival many times during the 1800s. So when church attendance started to wane and passion began to decline, a remnant felt burdened to pray. In 1903 a group of people pledged to spend one day each month praying for revival. One young man from this gathering, Evan Roberts, went on to ministry school, and it was there that God began to draw his heart toward his people back home. During one service he had a vision of being in the schoolroom in his hometown, where he was speaking to all of his childhood friends and acquaintances. The call to go home became stronger, but Roberts fought it, feeling ill-equipped and insecure. Eventually, however, he conceded and agreed to go back. When he arrived he called the young people to come together, and as he stood on the stage, he realized that what he saw was exactly as it had been in his vision. In this small, humble gathering, 12 people gave their lives to Jesus. Roberts started to reach out to more young people, but when their parents heard about what was going on, they didn't want to be left out! More and more gathered, with Roberts preaching unceasingly from morning to night. He was young, and what he said was simple. He was not an eloquent speaker, and yet God continued to move through him in a powerful way.

What was unique about the revival in Wales was that it was not merely led by sermons but also by song. The people loved to sing, and the Holy Spirit seemed to meet them in this way—with new songs, beautiful harmonies, and spontaneous worship that the whole assembly could follow even if there were no words on a screen or leaders to tell them what to do next. Roberts would move in these gatherings with great sensitivity, letting the Holy Spirit guide the proceedings rather than trying to create or follow his own agenda. Sometimes the people would sing for hours, or Roberts would be interrupted by a song in the middle of speaking and would join right in. Other times a spirit of repentance would fall, and people would give public confessions. Roberts was determined that the revival would not be about him—and in truth, it wasn't. Other men rose up, leading gatherings simultaneously across the nation. There simply were too many people for one man to reach. Even in places where no one was in charge, God would move powerfully. In the early stages, Roberts would pray for just a few more to be saved, but eventually his prayers got bigger. He began to prophesy that 100,000 people in Wales would be touched by the power of God—and even bigger, still, that the whole world would be affected by what God would do in their region. His words would come true. For two years revival was poured out over the people. Pubs shut down and courthouses emptied; people were no longer breaking the law or arguing with one another. Police departments had nothing to do, so they would join the singing and gather with the people. Churches were no longer just for Sunday mornings but were filled day and night with prayer, song, teaching, and confession. It was said that over 100,000 people gave their lives to Jesus, and still another 100,000 sleeping Christians reawakened and rededicated their lives to God. Citizens in other countries watched with hunger and began to pray for God to do such things in their own nations. And God, moved by the prayers of His people, would begin to answer.

VOCABULARY

EARLY READER
vow: *a promise*
immerse: *to fully get involved in something*

EARLY ELEMENTARY
immerse: *to fully get involved in something*
profitable: *makes money or is beneficial*

UPPER ELEMENTARY
profitable: *makes money or is beneficial*
beseech: *to ask for something in an urgent way*

MIDDLE SCHOOL
beseech: *to ask for something in an urgent way*
abhorrent: *truly terrible*

HIGH SCHOOL
abhorrent: *truly terrible*
doggedly: *in a determined manner*

HANDS-ON Activity

When the Roman Empire had to decide what to do about Luther, they gathered in an assembly that was called the Diet of Worms. *Diet* meant "assembly," and it was named *worms* because it was held in Worms, Germany. Have some fun by changing the meaning and eating an actual diet of worms—this could be noodles or even the candy variety. As you eat your snack, talk about what it might have been like to argue about what should be done to Luther.

Renaissance and Revival

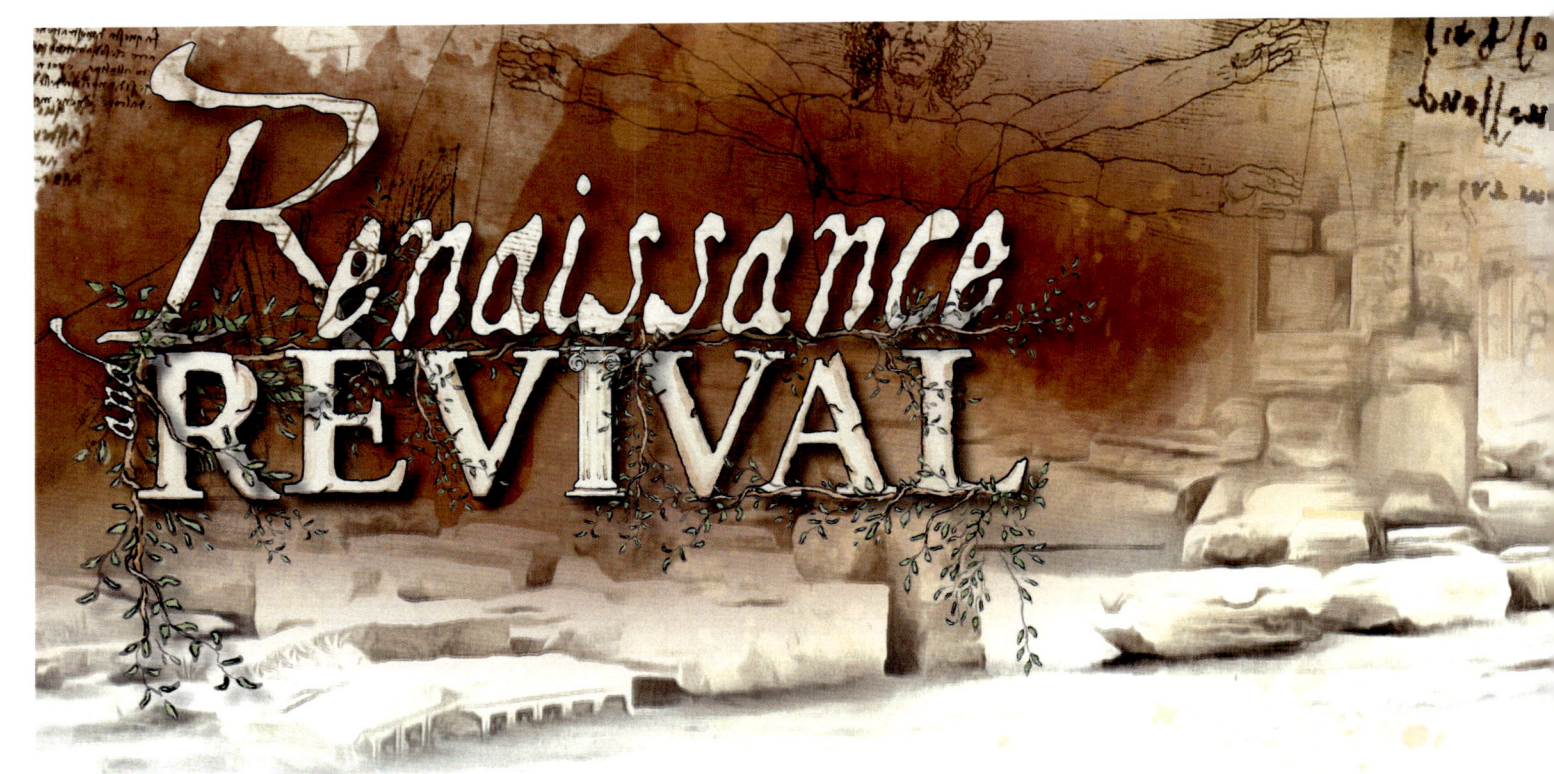

LESSON 11: WILLIAM TYNDALE

Throughout our study of the Renaissance era, we have seen the pioneering work of artists and ordinary businessmen, mapmakers and sailors, politicians and kings, and scholars and theologians. In fact it helps to think of this time period as a locomotive, with each important figure acting as an engine that propelled (or pulled) the cars forward. Like with your school subjects, everything that happened during the Renaissance was connected together to lead to one commonality: change. Can you imagine living during this time? The stakes were high. To be a reformer (whether in art, math, science, politics, theology, or anything else), one had to be willing to pay a great price. Great men and women risked **ridicule**, their jobs, and for some even their very lives to pursue what they believed. Many of these risk-takers would fade into obscurity as laughingstocks, only recognized for their genius long after they were gone. One man would pay the ultimate price—yet compared to anyone else, he would make one of the most significant contributions to the Protestant Reformation.

MEET WILLIAM TYNDALE

No one knows for certain when William Tyndale was born, although historians guess it was somewhere around 1492. He was an ordinary boy who lived in an ordinary household in England. His name doesn't even show up in public records until his enrollment at Oxford University when he was about 14 years old. He had a unique mind that was no less brilliant than some of the other inventors and forerunners of the Renaissance. His particular talent was in the arena of languages. They say that the more languages you learn, the more of them you are able to understand—almost like your brain is able to crack the codes. William spoke not two, not three, but *eight* languages: Hebrew, Greek, Latin, Italian, Spanish, French, German, and English. He gained his master's degree and went on to study theology at the University of Cambridge. It was there that his love for the scriptures was truly developed; he believed that God's word should be available to everyone—not just scholars. After his studies were completed, William was **ordained** as a priest and took a job as a tutor. And it was during this posting that his true calling would be revealed.

WILLIAM TYNDALE STATUE IN LONDON, UK

TEACHER'S GUIDE LESSON 11

WILLIAM TYNDALE

NOTEBOOKING/LAPBOOK *Alert*

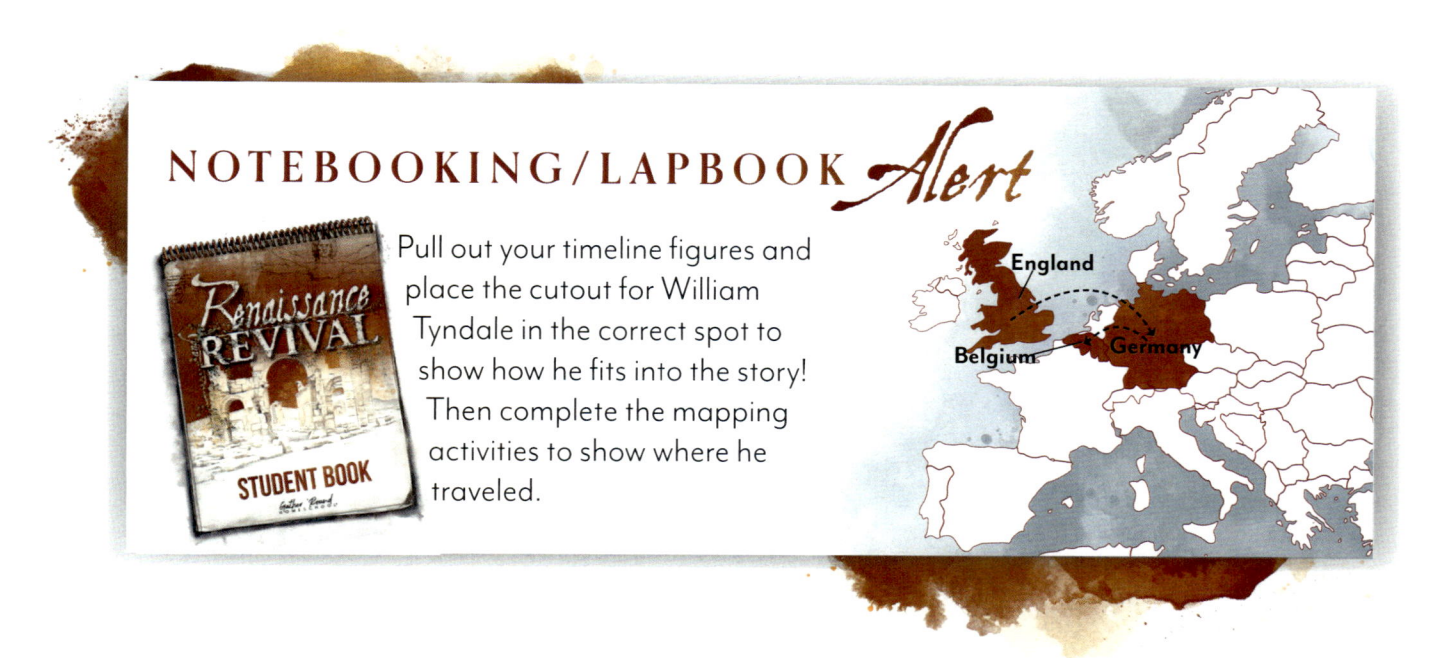

Pull out your timeline figures and place the cutout for William Tyndale in the correct spot to show how he fits into the story! Then complete the mapping activities to show where he traveled.

AN EXTRAORDINARY CHALLENGE

Different stories are told about the conversation that would forever change the course of William's life. Some say it happened while he was on a walk. Others say it took place at his employer's house during dinner one evening. Regardless of where he was when it occurred, when an educated individual made the statement, "We were better without God's law than the pope's,"[10] William knew there was a serious problem. The pope's authority was not higher than God's . . . if only the people could know Him for themselves! William responded with a promise—a threat even. He said that if God would spare his life and give him enough time, he would make it his personal goal to ensure that even the commoner would know more Scripture than the educated scholars of the day. His life's purpose became focused on one **trajectory**—to translate the Bible from its original languages (Greek and Hebrew) into modern-day English, which could be easily understood by anyone. However, this was strictly prohibited by the church. It saw English as rough and unsophisticated—not nearly as holy as Latin. How could the poetic words of the Holy Scriptures be **tainted**

WILLIAM TYNDALE

by the common language of the uneducated? There weren't even words in English for some of the original language. Truly, the English language seemed like it couldn't contain God's word without seriously changing its meaning. But the church greatly underestimated William, who as it turned out was uniquely equipped for the challenge. Like Shakespeare, Tyndale created new words that would become a part of our everyday speech. His understanding of the original Hebrew and Greek allowed him to manipulate the English language to even mimic some of the style and form of these ancient languages. When his first translations of the gospel were distributed, William was excommunicated and forced to flee. He would move to Germany where he would finish his translation of the New Testament and find support among the growing Lutheran movement.

TEACHER'S GUIDE LESSON 11   **WILLIAM TYNDALE**

With his New Testament complete, William would be forced to go on the run yet again, this time to Belgium, where he began to work on his translation of the Old Testament. Do you remember King Henry VIII and Thomas More? During this time More wrote multiple arguments against William, actively calling him out as a **heretic**. King Henry VIII, even though he no longer supported the Roman Catholic Church in public, also disagreed with William's work and was said to have sent commissions to root out Tyndale and bring him home for trial. Despite the threats and demands, William refused to stop what he believed was God's work. When he was about halfway through his translation of the Old Testament, he was befriended by a man named Henry Phillips, who would ultimately betray William by telling him to go out and disclosing to the authorities where he would be. Tyndale was imprisoned under the charge of being a Lutheran and was sentenced to death. He became a martyr—someone who is killed for following Jesus—and in his final breath he called out, "Lord! Open the King of England's eyes."[11] William never got to complete the work that he had died creating—nor did he get to see the effect of it. His translation was so groundbreaking that it would pave the way for the KJV Bible. Tyndale's version of the Bible was copied and ultimately smuggled into the homes of thousands of people just as he had dreamed, inviting ordinary believers into personal relationships with a God who had been previously far beyond their reach.

NOTEBOOKING/LAPBOOK Alert

Pull out your notebooking page or lapbook and complete the section to show what you learned about William Tyndale.

KOREAN REVIVALS

It is nearly impossible to study the history of revival and not notice the importance and power of prayer. But have you caught another one of the main "ingredients" that is required? Each revival brings with it an undertone—a flavor, even—of humility. This quality is seen in the confession of mistakes and a need for God, submission to God's plan over man's, and leaders who point to Jesus rather than to their own platforms—much like William Tyndale, who accepted life as an outcast and ultimately his own death in order to make God known. Revival in Korea began around the same time as the one in Wales with this very marker of humility. And it all started with one man who was willing—at the cost of his own **dignity**—to humble himself for the sake of the kingdom.

In the early-1900s, North Korea was very isolated and under intense persecution. Multiple missionaries (including one from Wales) had been martyred for their faith. In the midst of this dark and dismal reality, the local people and missionaries who lived in the area began to pray for God to move. Two women in particular began to meet regularly and called others to join them to seek the Lord. Out of this extraordinary prayer, a gathering was assembled, and a doctor from Canada, Dr. Robert Hardie (who lived in the area as a full-time missionary), was asked to be the keynote speaker. God would lead Hardie to publicly confess—something that he later described as being "deeply painful and humiliating."[12] Despite the cost to his pride, however, Dr. Hardie obeyed. He admitted that in his past 10 years of ministry, he had not seen any fruit, and he had not been full of the Holy Spirit. Even more shocking was his confession of a strong racial prejudice against the Korean people that he was working with. Can you imagine? Many of the missionaries gathered there were, in fact, Korean! Robert spoke from a place of brokenness, and the hearts of the people were moved. The Korean people in turn confessed that they had hated the doctor. One can only assume that Hardie probably had a far different message planned than what he presented. And yet he humbled himself and surrendered to the Holy Spirit, allowing God to move powerfully in the gathering. The missions conference became a meeting place for reconciliation, forgiveness, and healing. And it was in this tender soil that the Lord would begin to move . . . it was an appetizer of what was yet to come.

About three years later, in 1906, reports of the revival in Wales began to arrive in North Korea, and the people there were hungry to see and taste this type of change for themselves. In the city of Pyongyang, the missionaries decided to pray through every day of the holiday season for revival in their area. At that time there was an annual gathering early in the year that churches would send their leaders in the region to. For a while the meeting progressed as normal. Nothing special appeared to be happening, and there were some nights that the room felt spiritually dead—almost like there was a wall of opposition that the leaders were facing. But after a short sermon on January 14th, the people were invited to pray—and pray they did. All at once the assembly of hundreds of pastors and leaders began to pray in one voice, pouring out their hearts to God. This led to public confession and more reconciliation. When one leader came forward and humbly confessed his hatred toward one of the missionaries and asked for his forgiveness, something seemed to break. God's presence filled the room with such awe, wonder, and holiness that each man's sin seemed a burden too heavy to bear. These leaders would go home to their churches, carrying revival within them. For the next three years, a great movement broke out that started in the universities. Thousands would gather—sometimes walking hundreds of miles to meet. Despite great persecution, the church continued to grow in leaps and bounds, and hundreds of thousands of people gave their lives to Jesus. Many new churches were planted, and some of the largest churches in the world today are found in this nation because of the people who were willing to become "undignified"[13] according to the world so God's name would be glorified.

> If my people who are called by my name humble themselves, and pray and seek my face and turn from their wicked ways, then I will hear from heaven and will forgive their sin and heal their land.
> —2 Chronicles 7:14

VOCABULARY

EARLY READER
mimic: *to copy someone else's actions*
ridicule: *to make fun of someone*

EARLY ELEMENTARY
ridicule: *to make fun of someone*
dignity: *the quality of being respected*

UPPER ELEMENTARY
trajectory: *the path that something follows*
tainted: *ruined*

MIDDLE SCHOOL
tainted: *ruined*
ordained: *to be made a priest or pastor through a special ceremony*

HIGH SCHOOL
ordained: *to be made a priest or pastor through a special ceremony*
heretic: *someone who believes something that is the opposite of what is accepted or thought to be true*

HANDS-ON Activity

How well do you think you know the English language? Test your knowledge by seeing how many different ways you can write/communicate: "I was so happy to see you today." You might want to check out a thesaurus for this one!

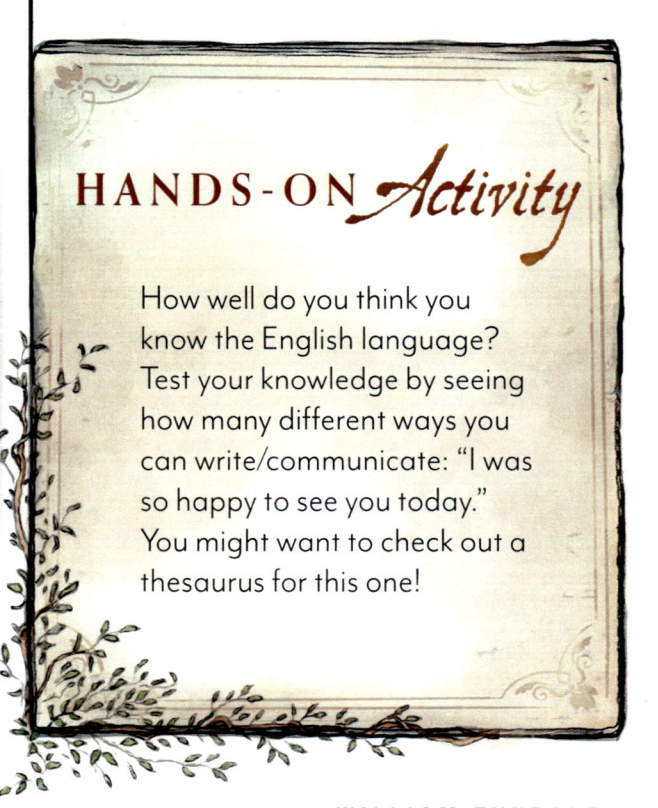

Renaissance and REVIVAL

LESSON 12: COPERNICUS

Nicolaus Copernicus was born in Poland on February 19, 1473. His parents were wealthy merchants but died when Nicolaus was young, leaving him and his siblings in the care of his uncle, an **aspiring** bishop. This uncle paved the way for Nicolaus to go to school and eventually get a job in the church. Copernicus went to quite a few universities, including a school in Poland and a number of different ones in Italy. There he studied all sorts of things like Greek, mathematics, economics, astronomy, and even medical science. He never finished a bachelor's degree in any of these areas; instead he moved from subject to subject and eventually gained his doctorate in canon law. After his uncle's death, Nicolaus moved home to Poland and served in his church as a canon, helping to take care of the church's affairs. Throughout his career he gave advice on economics; he even wrote an essay on how he would handle the **currency**. On his own time, however, he pursued his true passion: astronomy. His studies in Greek allowed him to be able to read some classic literature by ancient Greek scientists like Ptolemy. He began working on a manuscript called *On the Revolutions of the Heavenly Spheres*, which contained his theory of what would be coined the *heliocentric model*. Throughout most of his life, Copernicus was conspicuously silent about his ideas. Perhaps he was afraid of what these new theories would cost him, or maybe he was simply a perfectionist who wanted to have everything right before he shared it with others. When a young mathematician came to study under him, the boy showed Copernicus some of the new textbooks and the power of the new printing press, convincing his teacher to publish his manuscript for the world to see. Still Copernicus waited, continually adding to his work, concerned that his theory was not yet complete. The young pupil was finally successful, and Copernicus' book was published—just in time for Nicolaus to see the finished copy on his deathbed.

MONUMENT OF GREAT ASTRONOMER NICOLAUS COPERNICUS, TORUN, POLAND

TEACHER'S GUIDE LESSON 12

DID YOU KNOW? While the world remembers him as Copernicus, this is actually the Latin version of his name. His Polish name was Mikolaj Kopernik—it's kind of like how the name John is spelled *J-e-a-n* in French—but he chose to go by the Latin spelling of his name mainly because that was what most scientists did at the time. Changing one's name wasn't an uncommon practice throughout history, mainly because people didn't have to pay a fee and register with their nations like you do today. Kings often chose their own names when they were crowned, and many people who immigrated to new countries changed their names for easier pronunciation or because it helped them fit in more. What do you think? If you had to choose a new name, what would it be?

NOTEBOOKING/LAPBOOK Alert

Pull out your timeline figures and place the cutout for Nicolaus Copernicus in the correct spot to show how he fits into the story! Then mark *Poland* on the map to show where he was from.

THE HELIOCENTRIC MODEL

So what was this heliocentric model, and why was it so important? At this time in history, the mainstream belief of most scholars was that the Earth was the center of the universe, and that the Sun, planets, and stars all rotated around, well . . . them. Copernicus studied these models and believed that the math was incorrect. His manuscript laid out what he **meticulously** observed night after night: the constellations shifting positions in the sky. And from simply watching the heavens, he proposed a new theory. What if Ptolemy was wrong? What if the Earth actually made its way around the Sun, which stayed in one place? What if the stars didn't move, but rather it was our view of space that changed—something that would make sense if the Earth rotated as it orbited the Sun. Copernicus' equations could account for everything: day and night as well as seasons and years. His calculations weren't all entirely accurate. As he had **surmised**, there were a few small errors in his theory (for example he thought that the planets moved in exact circles, while modern calculations show them following more oval paths). But considering he didn't have a telescope, his ideas were revolutionary and far ahead of his time. His book would be like a diving board that other astronomers could leap off of, adding their own theories and discoveries to fill in the gaps. The world might not have been ready for what Nicolaus had to say—in fact the church forbade his book for a time—but like so many other Renaissance reformers, his contributions would change the face of science forever.

TEACHER'S GUIDE LESSON 12   **COPERNICUS**

GEOCENTRIC MODEL   **HELIOCENTRIC MODEL**

DID YOU KNOW? There are some people who still believe that Copernicus was wrong and that the original astronomers like Ptolemy were actually right. They argue that the Bible teaches a geocentric model (meaning the Earth is the center of the solar system, and the Sun and planets rotate around it) based primarily on Joshua 10:13a, which says, "And the sun stood still, and the moon stopped." However many scholars and scientists argue that this passage was written from the perspective of someone on Earth looking up at the sky and seeing the Sun stop its progress across the horizon—not speaking to the actual rotation of the solar system. What do you think? Talk about it as a family.

POLISH RENAISSANCE

Copernicus lived during the Polish Golden Age—his home country was not left untouched by the reform, style, culture, and ideas that were being forwarded from the south (namely Italy). Like how the Medici family helped forward the Italian Renaissance by sponsoring many artists, the Polish king, Sigismund I, brought artists from Italy to Poland and commissioned them to do work. Have you ever noticed that nations often compete to be the first or even the best at something—like the Space Race? There is a good reason for this competition . . . it's kind of like a big popularity contest. The better a nation performs (in sports, money, war, science, or anything else), the stronger it appears. More people might move there, invest their money there, or even send their young people to train or learn there. By the time that the Renaissance reached Poland, the race was on to see which country would be the best at, well, *all* of it. Which nation would produce the best artists? The only way to tell was to bring in masters to train up **protégés**. Which would contain the best scientific or mathematical minds? Schools and universities needed to be built and invested in so learning could flourish. At the end of the day, it was all about money. Whatever country had the most wealth would be able to compete in even more categories, and Poland was no small player. The king (and later his son) would commission artists to paint masterpieces and architects to remodel cathedrals and castles into a more classical style; they would also establish over 17 print houses so more literature could be published.

TEACHER'S GUIDE LESSON 12

SUNSET ON TOWN SQUARE IN ZAMOSC, POLAND.

One particular icon of this era was a city called Zamość *(zaim-ohsht)*, which was constructed by an Italian architect, Bernando Morando. All throughout the Renaissance, people had dreamt about the concept of the **"ideal** city." Philosophers like Thomas More imagined how a society could be set up, and architects like Leonardo imagined how it could be laid out. More than just imagining the beauty of the buildings, people came up with theories, designs, and plans for how the city could be structured for safety and efficiency. It was in Poland that the ideal eventually became a reality. Its inspiration? The *Vitruvian Man* that Leonardo had drawn (which is also the header of each of these lessons)! In Zamość the palace was the head, the main street was the spine, and the Academy and Cathedral were the lungs from which the city would get life. The city is still there today, a gem of the Renaissance and an amazing place to visit and see some of the classical architecture that the period was known for.

NOTEBOOKING/LAPBOOK *Alert*

What would an ideal city look like to you? Pull out your notebook or lapbook and complete the activity about the Polish Renaissance. If you want to, check out the resources page on the app for a virtual tour of Zamość to learn more!

KHASI HILLS REVIVAL

One of the most common outcomes of so many of these revivals was people feeling called to lay down their careers and go into full-time ministry. In some places seminary schools were full to the brim with the very real fruit of revival. A great number of people became missionaries, leaving their homes behind and following the call of God on their lives. This was especially evident in Wales. As revival poured out in waves, people also went out in waves, going to the farthest reaches of the world to share the gospel with unreached people groups. One area that many Welsh missionaries felt called to was India. In the 1800s this was a dangerous assignment. Many Indian people followed pagan gods and persecuted Christians. As with all revivals, the movement started with just a few people who felt compelled to pray for God to move. When news of the Welsh revival reached Khasi Hills, it stirred up hope, and believers committed to praying every night. The air was thick with anticipation—so much so that when a Sunday morning service was about to end in its usual manner, one man was deeply disappointed. He prayed out loud, asking God to bless the people in the congregation like He did their brothers and sisters in Wales. The cry of his heart was picked up by others until the whole assembly was moved to fervently pray, *Us too, Lord!* Into this hunger, need, and deep faith, the Spirit of the Lord was poured out. Those who were at the service brought their stories to their home churches, sparking hope among their own people. Almost like the days of old, people laid their offerings on the altar, confessing their sins and offering their humble faith. And the Holy Spirit came like a fire, setting their offerings ablaze.

The children were not unaffected. In many churches it was the prayer of one young person that would spark something among the whole congregation. In some regions the children started their own prayer meetings, often crying out to God for hours. Many of these kids went out and shared the gospel in the open markets and to their friends and neighbors with incredible results. There was no single leader, no great speaker. As the people hungered and contended, as they prayed and expected . . . God moved. Many pagans received dreams and visions directly from the Lord that led to their conversions. The power of God was unmistakable. In some meetings people felt a shaking; others experienced a powerful wind; and still others saw flames of fire like at Pentecost. In one village church, people saw a great light coming from within the church, and they went rushing in with great concern, thinking that the building had been struck by lightning. But inside of the church, the believers themselves were each surrounded by flashes of light—and those who had hardened their hearts against God were deeply affected. Like what happened in Wales, many people would lay down their lives as a result of their encounters, spreading revival all throughout India and stirring up hunger in other nations . . . *Us too, Lord!*

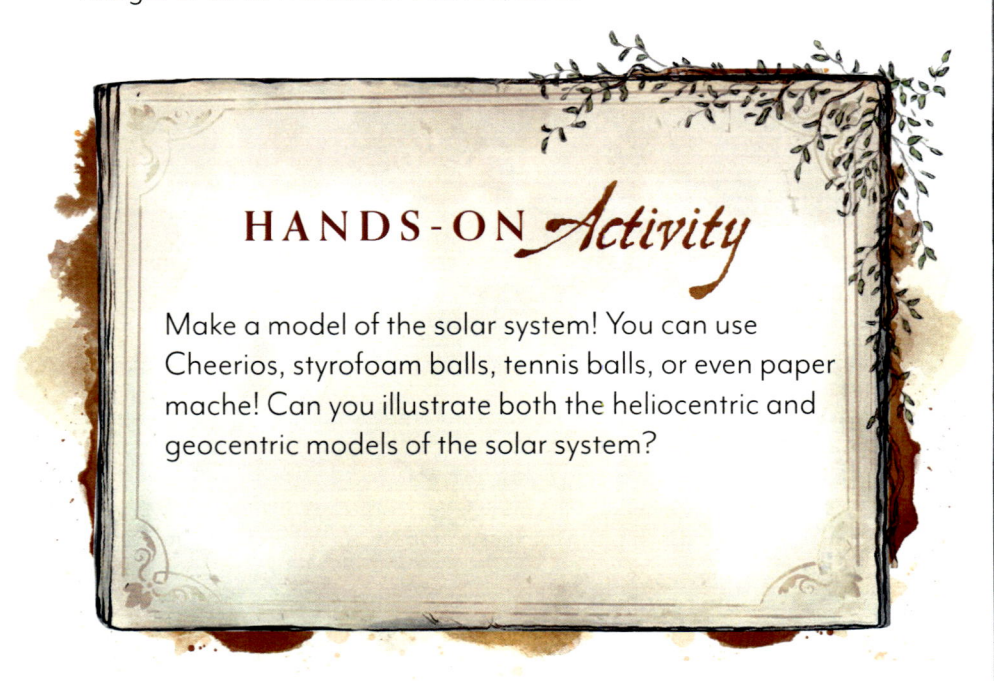

HANDS-ON *Activity*

Make a model of the solar system! You can use Cheerios, styrofoam balls, tennis balls, or even paper mache! Can you illustrate both the heliocentric and geocentric models of the solar system?

VOCABULARY

EARLY READER
currency: *the official paper money and coins of a country*
ideal: *a perfect example of something*

EARLY ELEMENTARY
ideal: *a perfect example of something*
aspire: *to work really hard at something that you want to do or be*

UPPER ELEMENTARY
aspire: *to work really hard at something that you want to do or be*
meticulous: *paying careful attention to every detail*

MIDDLE SCHOOL
meticulous: *paying careful attention to every detail*
protégé: *a young student who is taught a skill by someone who is well-known in that industry*

HIGH SCHOOL
protégé: *a young student who is taught a skill by someone who is well-known in that industry*
surmise: *to make an opinion or guess about something without having any evidence*

Renaissance and Revival

LESSON 13: CATHERINE DE' MEDICI

We've talked about a lot of men and how they contributed to the Renaissance, but women were just as influential—even if sometimes they only worked in the background to help nudge things in the right direction. At this time in history, it is important to remember that the roles of men and women were significantly different than they are today. Women were expected to bear children and keep the house. Unlike boys they were not sent to school to be educated, and they did not work outside of the home. They were often married off by the time they were teenagers in order to secure family ties and positions. Not every girl was lucky enough to get married because it actually cost money to do so! Each marriage required a **dowry**. The better the match, the higher the dowry was expected to be, and payment was often made in the form of properties, homes, household goods, and even money (or the cancellation of debts). A royal marriage might have even come with an entire city—how's *that* for a wedding gift? For families that couldn't afford dowries, the women might have been sent to convents to become nuns—kind of like the female equivalent of monks. It might sound less exciting than getting married, but being a nun could actually be pretty great. It meant that the woman was free to study and learn and did not have to face the risks of childbirth or the fear of being married off to someone who might not treat her well. Some nuns even became painters—though their works were less well known, and the women were not commissioned (or paid) like their male counterparts were. While a *Renaissance man* was someone who made extraordinary advances in his area of expertise, a *Renaissance woman* also did that *and* battled against the cultural view that a woman should stick to her position. Women like Joan of Arc (who broke the status quo and led a revolution) or Felice Della Rovere (who despite being an illegitimate child of the pope, was well educated and incredibly powerful) defied all the odds that were stacked up against them. Let's take a look at one Renaissance woman who refused to stay in the box that society wanted her to fit into.

Teacher's Guide **LESSON 13**

MEET CATHERINE DE' MEDICI

Do you remember the Medici family back in Florence? We left off with Lorenzo the Magnificent, a **patron** of the arts who was heavily involved in the politics of the city. His grandson, Lorenzo II, would have a daughter who would rise in rank and power, proving that the Medici name was a family of merchants no longer. Her mother died when she was only a few weeks old, and her father passed shortly thereafter, leaving Catherine de' Medici an orphan by the time she was only a month old. She had a difficult childhood, being passed around from relative to relative and even facing threats. Her uncle was the pope, and he brought her to a convent where she was raised and taught by nuns until she was old enough to be married—which during the Renaissance was quite young indeed. At the tender age of 14, Catherine entered into an arranged marriage with a prince from France named Henry. This unimaginable match only happened because France hoped to gain favor with the pope. It was said that when Catherine first arrived at court, she felt insecure because she was short (under five feet tall). So she came to her wedding as the first woman in recorded history to wear high heels—the beginning of a long line of trends that can be traced back to this history-making woman. Despite the fact that she wasn't particularly liked among the people or the court, she carved her mark in history by any means necessary.

PORTRAIT OF CATHERINE DE' MEDICI BY HENRI SAUVAGE

NOTEBOOKING/LAPBOOK *Alert*

Pull out your timeline figures and place the cutout for Catherine de' Medici in the correct spot to show how she fits into the story!

When Henry's older brother died, it put him next in line for the throne. And in 1547 Catherine became queen—though it wouldn't mean much for some time. The king had another woman, Diane, whom he had loved before entering into his arranged marriage. He preferred her over Catherine (even showing his affection for her by allowing her to write letters and sign them as *HenriDiane*). For 10 long years, Catherine's position was **tenuous**. Her uncle had died giving her no real connections, and she had remained childless, which made her altogether too disposable. But after the birth of a royal heir, Francis, she went on to have nine more children, thus fulfilling her duty. When Henry died from wounds during a jousting competition, his eldest son Francis II became king at only 15 years old, and that's when things began to change. Seeing an opportunity to rise in power, Catherine brought a false accusation against her biggest competition; in doing so she made herself the best (and really only) choice for regent and instilled fear in many at the court who might have dared to cross her. Francis II ruled only two years before he died, leaving his 10-year-old brother to take his place and once again putting Catherine in the role of regent. This wasn't an easy time to rule because of the great divisions between Catholics and Protestants. Many would say that the Queen did a poor job in her role; she was even blamed for orchestrating a brutal massacre of the Huguenots (Protestants). When her third and favorite son took the throne, Catherine's power was waning. People had lost confidence in the family, and change was on the horizon.

TEACHER'S GUIDE LESSON 13

CHANGING FRANCE

So what did Catherine contribute to the Renaissance? Like the rest of her family, she was a committed patron of the arts, seeing them as an opportunity to both keep the nation current and to help distract the court from looking too closely at the growing unrest. When her third son became king, she sponsored the ballet to perform for him. She also invested in architecture, adding a wing to the royal palace and building the Tuileries Garden, a World Heritage site that attracts many visitors today. This garden sprawls across the city of Paris, ending at the Louvre. Throughout history these beautiful grounds were carefully cared for and remodeled—at one point they were even filled with carnival rides and performers! Catherine also brought some of her favorite recipes to court, and while the dishes (such as onion soup and even macarons) were originally from her home in Italy, they would later become signature French staples! She even brought the first forks to France and taught the people how to use them—much to their initial frustration. She might not have been able to successfully navigate the religious war that was constantly simmering underneath the surface, but for better or worse, she established her **foothold** in a new country that didn't necessarily want her—which was pretty impressive . . . for a woman that is.

NOTABLE ARCHITECTURE

Have you ever heard of the Louvre? This is the largest and most-visited museum in the world today, and its history can be traced back to precisely this period of time. Though it was originally built as a military fortification to protect Paris from the invading Viking armies, the growth of the city made the Louvre no longer useful for defense. Over time, different monarchs had different plans for the building—it was constantly under construction—but they lacked a consistent vision and style. When her husband died, Catherine de' Medici saw an opportunity. She commissioned a new palace (called the Tuileries Palace) to be built in the gardens a short distance away from the Louvre. It would later be connected to the Louvre with a long building, making Catherine an unmistakable part of the museum. As time went on, the royal houses lost interest in the structure, which was becoming the heart of the city. They wanted to get away and have their own space, and so the Louvre was used to house artists instead. It has had many different purposes as well as numerous facelifts through the years, serving as a school, home, palace, and more! Eventually it was given a singular role as an art museum, and today it holds some of the most famous paintings and sculptures in the world, including many pieces from the Renaissance (such as the *Mona Lisa*).

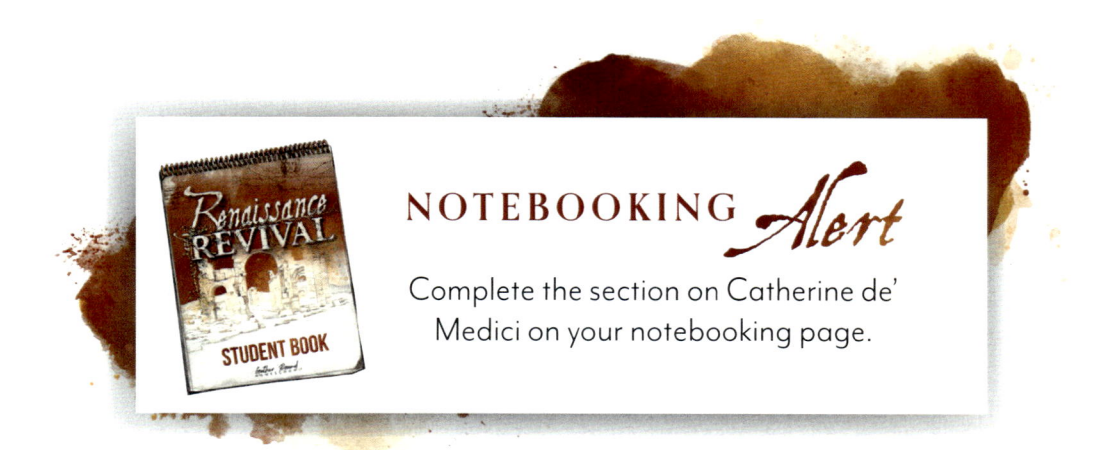

NOTEBOOKING Alert

Complete the section on Catherine de' Medici on your notebooking page.

AERIAL VIEW OF LOUVRE MUSEUM, PARIS, FRANCE

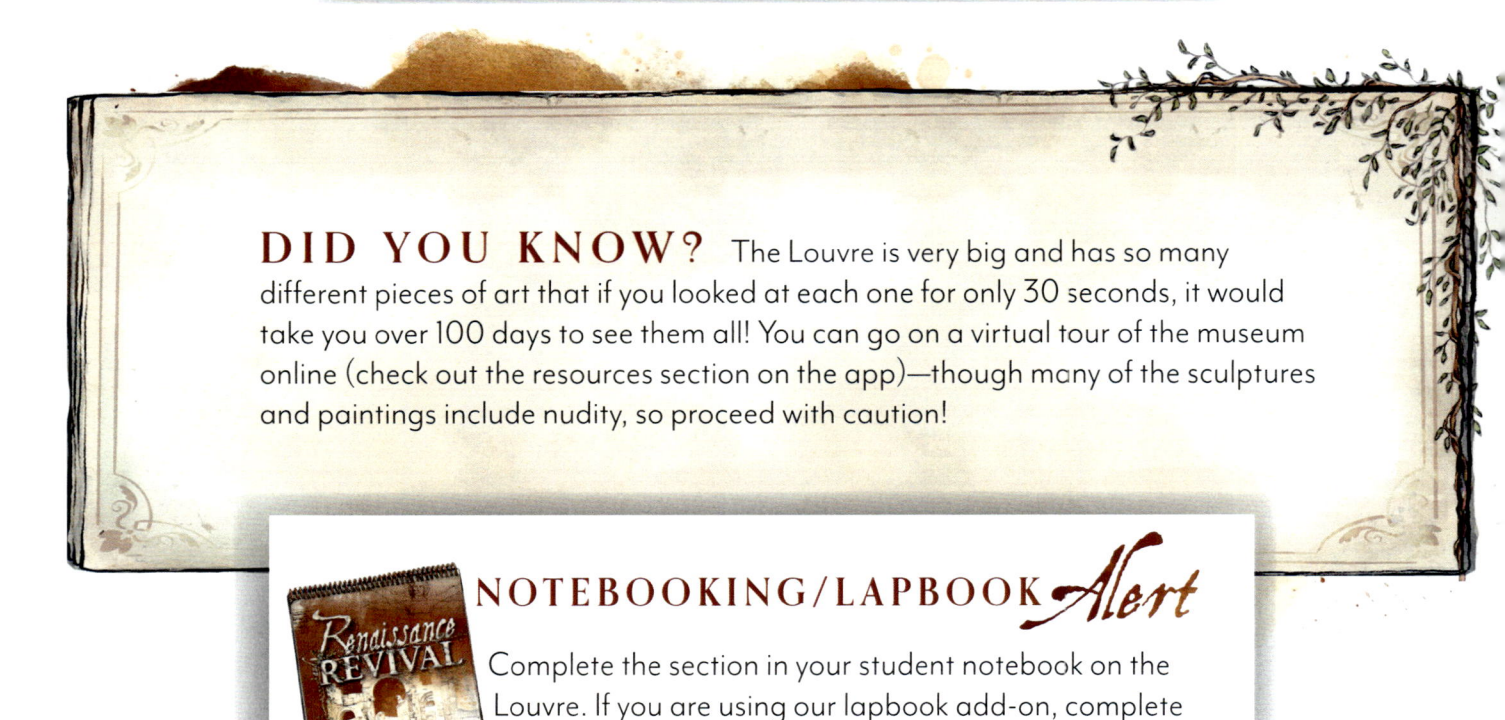

DID YOU KNOW? The Louvre is very big and has so many different pieces of art that if you looked at each one for only 30 seconds, it would take you over 100 days to see them all! You can go on a virtual tour of the museum online (check out the resources section on the app)—though many of the sculptures and paintings include nudity, so proceed with caution!

NOTEBOOKING/LAPBOOK *Alert*

Complete the section in your student notebook on the Louvre. If you are using our lapbook add-on, complete the Louvre activity and add it to your lapbook!

LATTER RAIN REVIVAL

Each and every revival that we have studied in this unit so far faced some sort of **opposition**. There have always been those who stood against the movements, writing them off as emotionalism or even heretical. The truth is, sometimes the signs and wonders that accompany an outpouring of the Holy Spirit are uncomfortable to watch and hard to explain. It is also important to note that the devil is also known as the "father of lies," and for every thing that is real and true, there are also often counterfeits. Discerning what is right when it comes to supernatural realities is not easy, especially if you can't be there to see the context and prayerfully ask the Lord for wisdom. During many of the revivals that we have learned about, the critics who went to see things for themselves were touched in the same ways as the other people there, and they could not deny that God was at work. However, other movements were sometimes exploited or even twisted by the enemy or by man's own prideful ambition. This tension has always existed, and unfortunately it has created great division within the church. Let's take a look at one revival that was highly debated.

In 1947 God was moving powerfully in North America with a healing revival that was taking place. Giant tent meetings were being held, and many people were touched by the Holy Spirit. Meanwhile, a ministry in Canada was facing opposition for their emphasis on the signs and wonders of God. In response to the disagreement, a split happened, and the group moved to North Battleford, Saskatchewan, where an orphanage and school were opened. After hearing about the revivals that had been happening on the West Coast, two of the leaders of the North Battleford movement went to Vancouver to see it for themselves. What they saw lit a fire within them; as thousands gathered, sickness was healed, and the city was forever changed. They came back hungry for God to move in their region, heralding the cry of revivalists everywhere: *Us too, Lord!* The men led their school in intentional study, prayer, and fasting through the winter to prepare for what they believed would come. They were so certain that God would move that they actually planned a four-day gathering with extended services—the anticipation was **palpable**! By the second day, the Holy Spirit came upon the group. Many young people were called into ministry, prophecies went forth, sicknesses were healed, and God's presence was thick in the room—the peace was undeniable. And this was just the beginning.

EXTRA! EXTRA!

May 1947

GREAT SPIRITUAL AWAKENING

COME AND SEE

REVIVAL

STARTING MONDAY,
MAY 9, 2:30 AND 7:30 DAILY

Calvary Temple
123 NORTH LAKE STREET

WITH
GEO. E. HAWTIN
E.H. HAWTIN
M.E. KIRKPATRICK
of North Battleford, Canada

TEACHER'S GUIDE LESSON 13 — CATHERINE DE' MEDICI

Throughout the spring many people visited the school to receive prayer, and reports came back of an increased passion for prayer and fasting in these people's home churches as a direct result of them visiting the school. But the leaders felt that there was more to come. In preparation for their yearly camp meeting, the directors organized a 12-day fast, and they were not disappointed. People from all over the continent attended the event, and many were forever changed. Like revivals do, the movement spread. The North Battleford ministry team was invited to various cities to speak and pray, and God moved powerfully in those places too. Eventually other churches and ministries carried the revival torch through the United States, where God continued to stir up revival. Many mainstream churches, however, rejected the movement. As we learned with Martin Luther, we all see in part; none of us is perfect, and the enthusiasm of the movement did not come without some highly-debated theology. Some were known to give strong prophetic words of direction, such as divinely-appointed marriages (which they did not believe could be questioned). Their idea that the churches should come under the apostles and prophets was offensive to many, while others didn't agree with the idea of modern-day prophecy or the apostolic at all. Talk about it as a family. What do you think? Have you ever seen God move in a way that was hard to explain? Why do you think that it's important to go somewhere for yourself to hear, see, and understand before judging a ministry or movement?

HANDS-ON *Activity*

Make an art museum at home! Create some art pieces—paintings, sculptures, etc.—that you'd like to put on display. Then invite your friends or family members to walk through your museum!

VOCABULARY

EARLY READER
patron: *someone who supports artists with money*
palpable: *able to be felt*

EARLY ELEMENTARY
palpable: *able to be felt*
foothold: *a solid position that allows one to move forward*

UPPER ELEMENTARY
foothold: *a solid position that allows one to move forward*
opposition: *anything that goes against a specific opinion or person*

MIDDLE SCHOOL
opposition: *anything that goes against a specific opinion or person*
dowry: *money or property that a woman and her family give to her husband when they marry*

HIGH SCHOOL
dowry: *money or property that a woman and her family give to her husband when they marry*
tenuous: *uncertain*

TEACHER'S GUIDE LESSON 13 — CATHERINE DE' MEDICI

Renaissance and Revival

LESSON 14: QUEEN MARY I

Some people hear the name Queen Mary and think of the wrong person, as this was a popular name during the Renaissance. Mary, Queen of Scots, was Catherine de' Medici's daughter-in-law. She grew up in the French court and married Francis—Henry and Catherine's oldest son. But this is not the same queen as the one in this lesson. Our story today will take us back to England to Henry VIII and his first child, Mary. You may remember that in order to wed Anne Boleyn, King Henry had to first find a way to **annul** his marriage with Mary's mother. He did this with a proclamation that made him head of the Church of England and denounced his daughter, Mary, as his heir. After secretly marrying Anne, Mary's childhood became more dangerous. Her mother was sent away, and she was not permitted to see her; she spent a good deal of time locked away essentially on house arrest—hidden from the king's sight and cast out of court until the arrival of Jane Seymour—who convinced her new husband to reconcile with his daughter.

Having been raised Catholic, Mary did not support her father's break from the church, and her beliefs made her a big problem for the monarch. When her father died, Mary's half-brother, Edward, took the king's place. He was only nine years old at the time and relied heavily on his advisors to help him rule. Raised Protestant, he saw Mary as a threat and once again declared her illegitimacy to the throne. When he was only 15 years old, Edward grew gravely ill. Not wanting England to fall back into Catholic hands, he created a plan to make his cousin, Lady Jane Grey, the queen after his death—though this scheme was ultimately unsuccessful. After hearing of Edward's death, Mary gathered her supporters and usurped the throne, executing both Jane and her husband and taking her rightful place by force in 1553.

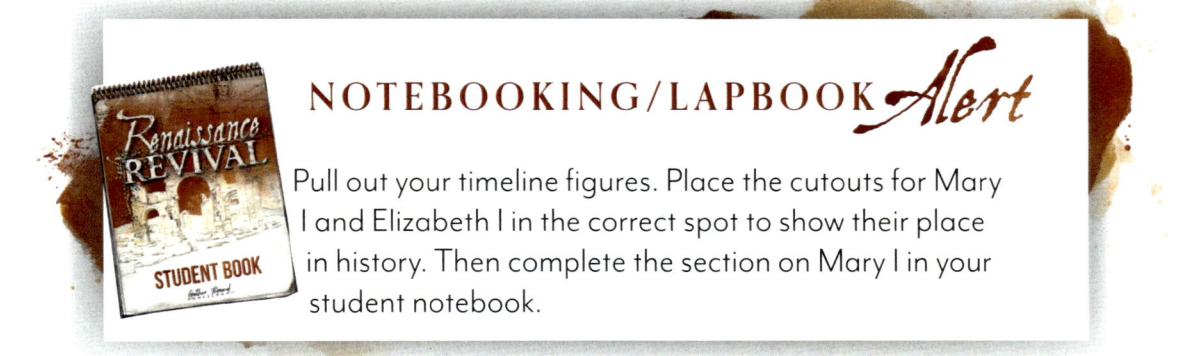

NOTEBOOKING/LAPBOOK Alert

Pull out your timeline figures. Place the cutouts for Mary I and Elizabeth I in the correct spot to show their place in history. Then complete the section on Mary I in your student notebook.

BLOODY MARY

For the first time in England's history, a queen was crowned not through marriage but as a rightful heir, which is known as being a *queen regnant*. While this was not unheard of in history (Have you ever heard of the Queen of Sheba in the Bible?), it was **unprecedented** throughout most of Europe. As a devout Catholic, Mary's first order of business was to undo what her father and brother had done. As soon as the crown was placed on her head, she became—by default—the supreme head of the Church of England (something that she had no desire to be). She refused the position and instead gave it back to the pope, reinstating Catholic bishops and making a bold statement: England was no longer a Protestant country. To restore religious order, she brought back the abandoned heresy laws—if you were not a professing Catholic like your queen, it was an act of **treason** punishable by death. Like Saul in the New Testament, Mary was **zealous** and absolutely convinced that she was doing God's holy work. She stood staunchly by her beliefs, resulting in over 300 Protestants being burned at the stake. Her brutality led to the nickname for which she would go down in history—Bloody Mary.

MARY TUDOR, QUEEN OF ENGLAND BY ANTHONIS MOR

NOW WHAT?

After taking the crown and dealing with the religious dissension, Mary had a new problem to solve, as her father had many wives during his lifetime but only three legitimate children: Edward (who had died), Elizabeth (Anne Boleyn's daughter), and of course Mary. In the beginning Elizabeth supported her sister, even joining her in London to celebrate her coronation. But as events began to unfold, the sisters' relationship became more and more strained, with Mary being an unapologetic Catholic and Elizabeth having been raised Protestant. Eventually a **plot** to overthrow Mary was uncovered, and her sister seemed the likely culprit. Elizabeth was arrested so there could be an investigation to find out if she was guilty. At the Tower of London, Elizabeth had access to only a few rooms but was allowed daily walks in the gardens where she was questioned and carefully watched. Eventually the leads came to a dead-end, and she was released, as there was no proof found of her involvement in the **coup**.

Mary still had a problem. Any leader must both build for today *and* think about tomorrow. Who would take over if she were to die? At this point the queen was unmarried and had no children of her own. The only true heir to the throne was Elizabeth, a ruler who would undoubtedly ping-pong the nation back to Protestant beliefs. In an attempt to secure the throne for generations, Mary married Philip II, the king of Spain. Despite her best efforts, however, she remained childless and died only a few years after her wedding. There was no other choice but to name Elizabeth the rightful queen of England.

DID YOU KNOW? A *coronation* is the official ceremony held to install a monarch with his or her powers as king or queen. In England this ceremony comes with a lot of traditions that date back thousands of years. During a coronation, the up-and-coming king or queen makes a public vow to serve God as well as the people of their country. Throughout the years different objects like crowns and scepters have been used on this occasion, but some other elements have remained the same for centuries. For example, a coronation spoon is used to anoint the new monarch with holy oil, a ritual that dates back to biblical times. The same spoon has been a part of the service since the 12th century—it was even used for the most recent coronation of King Charles III in May of 2023. Every ceremony up until Queen Elizabeth I's was performed completely in Latin. She was the first monarch to request that portions of the service be spoken in English so the people would be able to understand what she was promising them. Complete the section about coronations in your lapbook or on your notebooking page.

HEBRIDES REVIVAL

Do you remember the island of Lewis? This was where the Gaelic schools began to use Bibles as their textbooks, resulting in a powerful move of God that swept through the villages. Lewis is an island above Scotland and is part of an archipelago (or group of islands) called Hebrides *(heb-ruh-dees)*. We find ourselves back here in 1949 as a direct result of two old women who longed for more.

Peggy and Christine Smith were two sisters who were in their 80s—one was blind, and the other was bent over with arthritis. These women were grieved by the state of their church, and when the Lord laid on their hearts Isaiah 44:3a ("For I will pour water on the thirsty land, and streams on the dry ground"), they got on their knees to pray that His word would come to pass. A few times a week, they prayed in the wee hours of the night, starting at 10:00 p.m. and ending about 3:00 a.m. After a few weeks, Peggy (the blind sister) had a vision of their church being crowded with young people, and the sisters felt sure that it would happen soon, so they reached out to their pastor and told him that revival was coming. The women asked him to gather with the church leadership team to pray at the same time as they did every Tuesday and Friday night. The pastor listened, and other churches also began to pray afresh for God to move despite the long, cold winter and (in some places where they gathered) lack of heat. One by one, people began to sense that the Lord was extending an invitation: "Ask me for revival." And so . . . they did.

TEACHER'S GUIDE LESSON 14 **QUEEN MARY I**

There came a night when one of the pastors read from Psalm 24:3–5 and felt convicted. How could they be praying for revival if they didn't have clean hands and pure hearts? At 3:00 a.m. God's presence fell—not just on the people who were present at the meeting but also on others who were awake and praying at the same time. In fact, when the intercessors went outside, they found that the village was very much awake. Some people were outside crying out to the Lord, while others had their lights on in their homes because they couldn't sleep. Peggy sent for her pastor again, this time telling him that there was someone he was supposed to invite to preach. The minister reached out to a young man named Duncan Campbell but was turned down; Campbell had other plans. When Peggy heard this news, she seemed completely unconcerned, saying that Duncan would be there within two weeks. It just so happened that his plans were canceled, and 10 days later he arrived on the island of Lewis, where he was asked to go straight to the church to preach at 9:00 p.m.! Three hundred people gathered that first night, and the service commenced with nothing out of the ordinary—though an awareness of God's presence was thick in the room. The service ended at 10:45 p.m., and everyone other than Campbell and one young deacon went home. The deacon turned to Campbell, with all surety said that God would break through at any moment, and he started to pray. Only 15 minutes later, the back door of the church opened, and someone called for them to come and see the crowd that was gathering. The people started to stream in. It was a revival service with an unprecedented start time (12:00 a.m.) that was by invitation only. The Spirit of God drew people from all walks of life into the room until there were no seats left. The leaders discovered later that many of the people present had come from a dance being held nearby. God's presence had fallen right at the moment the young deacon had started praying, and the people ran to the church. Many more villagers were in bed but suddenly found themselves getting up and dressed to go to church. Everyone was there not by accident but rather by the sovereign hand of God. The service continued until 4:00 a.m., though there was no real "service" at all. People spontaneously prayed and sang scripture, being ministered to by the Holy Spirit.

Exhausted from his travels and a nearly all-night service, Campbell went to get some sleep, but on his way he was asked to go to the police station where 300 people had spontaneously gathered as well. Along the whole walk there, people were kneeling along the road and crying out to God. At the police station, Campbell saw buses full of people who had come from all around but weren't really sure why they were there. Again, no sermon was necessary, as God Himself touched the hearts of those gathered with His presence and a sense of conviction. Campbell remained in the area for five weeks, preaching at all hours of the day and night. The revival would continue to spread, not just across the island of Lewis but also on the surrounding islands as well. All throughout the revival, people like Peggy and Christine stayed in their homes and interceded so the movement might continue. There were many incredible stories of God bringing His people and then restoring them to Himself. No one knows for certain how many were saved because the leaders didn't want to fall into the sin of pride by counting souls for their own legacy. But the prayers of two little old ladies would come to pass, and nothing would ever be the same.

DID YOU KNOW? Peggy and Christine Smith's niece, Mary Anne Smith MacLeod, immigrated to the United States and married a man named Frederick Trump. She would become the mother of none other than the 45th president of the United States, Donald Trump, who was named after a young man who had a great impact on her life during the revival on the island of Lewis. In fact, President Trump inherited Peggy and Christine's Bible, which carried the scribbles and prayers of two incredible women who were used by God in an amazing way.

TEACHER'S GUIDE LESSON 14

HANDS-ON *Activity*

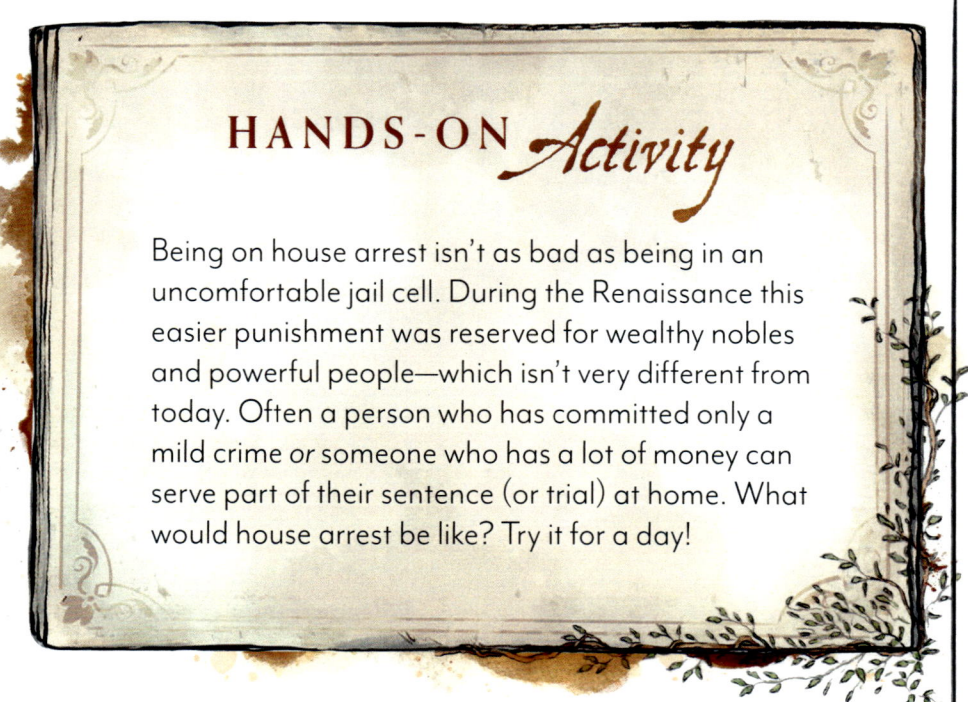

Being on house arrest isn't as bad as being in an uncomfortable jail cell. During the Renaissance this easier punishment was reserved for wealthy nobles and powerful people—which isn't very different from today. Often a person who has committed only a mild crime *or* someone who has a lot of money can serve part of their sentence (or trial) at home. What would house arrest be like? Try it for a day!

VOCABULARY

EARLY READER
plot: *a plan*
zealous: *very committed to a person or idea*

EARLY ELEMENTARY
zealous: *very committed to a person or idea*
coup: *a secret plan to try to take a ruler's place*

UPPER ELEMENTARY
coup: *a secret plan to try to take a ruler's place*
annul: *to bring an end to something*

MIDDLE SCHOOL
annul: *to bring an end to something*
treason: *betrayal*

HIGH SCHOOL
treason: *betrayal*
unprecedented: *not done before*

LESSON 15: RELIGIOUS WARS

We've talked a lot about the Protestant Reformation, and that's because it was one of the driving forces during the Renaissance. People were so certain of their beliefs that they were willing to die for them, and the religious war that took place was long, bloody, and had a huge impact on culture and politics. The Catholic Church initially tried to deal with the Reformation through warnings and excommunications. But despite the Church's best efforts to stop the movement, the ideas spread like wildfire, and the Roman Inquisition was established. Some people hoped for unity, seeking to bridge the ever-growing gap between Protestants and Catholics. Others sought a clear division as they tried to establish something new entirely. Like opening a can of worms, it seemed impossible to go back to the way things were. Today we'll review the Protestant Reformation as a whole along with the response of the Catholic Church in order to make our very own timeline of events and see how it all fit together.

WHAT NOW?

The Reformation was triggered by Martin Luther's posting of his 95 Theses in 1517—though there were many other people (like Erasmus) who were beginning to express concerns over some of the Church's theology long before that. In 1521 Luther was summoned to the Diet of Worms, a meeting to discuss his claims and to give him an opportunity to **recant**. During his questioning he stated that he would not change his mind unless someone could show him in scripture where he was wrong. His refusal led to an **edict** that ultimately started the religious war of the Renaissance. Luther was declared an enemy of the state, his works were banned, and his ideas were labeled as heretical, putting anyone who supported them at risk of punishment from the church. Luther escaped and went into hiding, but the line had been drawn in the sand, and the Catholic Church's problem was far from solved.

NOTEBOOKING/LAPBOOK Alert

Add it to the Protestant Reformation timeline.

- 1517 95 Theses
- 1521 Diet of Worms

The Edict of Worms seemed to have very little effect. Luther continued to write, and people continued to follow and advance his teachings. The Catholic Church saw these ideas as a threat, and as they watched them **pervade** the continent, one pope would make a decided move toward clarity. Pope Paul III (born Alessandro Farnese) had a diverse education, even studying at Lorenzo the Magnificent's house under many of the humanist teachers that were brought in to tutor the Medici children. When Alessandro was elected as pope in 1534, he found himself smack-dab in the middle of a crisis—but one that he felt well-prepared to handle. He decided to hold a series of meetings that would later become known as the Counter-Reformation (or Catholic Reformation).

COUNCIL OF TRENT AND THE ROMAN INQUISITION

Pope Paul III determined that in order to help soothe the religious unrest, an **assembly** was needed to address the growing concerns against the Catholic Church. The other cardinals did not agree with him, and it would take over 10 years for the pope to finally get his wishes. He started with the Colloquy of Regensburg in 1541. The ultimate goal of this meeting was to reunite the church by coming up with a compromise, which was brought to both the Pope and Luther, but both refused to accept it. With unity seeming to be out of grasp, Pope Paul III established the Roman Inquisition in 1542, a movement meant to help root out heretics and heretical materials. The Pope also worked to establish a new meeting (known as the Council of Trent) among the Catholic Church in 1545. This group would meet many times over the next 18 years, focusing primarily on the two subjects of corruption and the Protestant Reformation. The truth could not be denied: during the Middle Ages, things had decidedly gone downhill. The council implemented new rules to help avoid some of the problems that had been happening in the Church. While it still believed in indulgences, it made strict guidelines for issuing them and required bishops to keep records about them and report them so they would not be misused. The council also addressed misconduct and gave bishops more oversight of individual churches. But as for the beliefs of the Protestants, the group refused to budge. Let's take a look at some of the differences at the time.

> **NOTEBOOKING/LAPBOOK Alert**
> Add it to the Protestant Reformation timeline.
> - 1541 Colloquy of Regensburg
> - 1542 Roman Inquisition
> - 1545 Council of Trent

PROTESTANT BELIEFS
- Scripture is the ultimate authority
- Saved in Christ through faith alone
- Did not agree with indulgences
- Did not agree with purgatory
- No Apocrypha
- Bible should be available in people's native languages
- Imputed righteousness

CATHOLIC BELIEFS
- Scripture and tradition hold equal authority
- Saved by both faith and works
- Believed that indulgences held power
- Believed in purgatory
- Apocrypha
- Only the Latin Vulgate accepted
- Infused righteousness

NOTEBOOKING/LAPBOOK Alert

Pull out your timeline and add the cutout for the Council of Trent.

COUNCIL OF TRENT, PAINTING IN THE MUSEO DEL PALAZZO DEL BUONCONSIGLIO

This brings us to the second purpose of the council: to **refute** the Protestant Reformation and clarify where the Church stood on these and other issues. To enforce its stance, the group put forth the *Index Librorum Prohibitorum* (the Index of Prohibited Books) in 1563. This list included authors such as Erasmus and Luther as well as anyone else that might have been perceived as being in conflict with Catholic beliefs. This essentially meant that it was illegal and heretical to own an English or German Bible (or one written in anything other than Latin), along with any books or pamphlets written by the authors on the list. Those who disagreed with or rebelled against the order were at risk for excommunication or even death (depending on who was in power). It was certainly a dangerous time in history to disagree!

NOTEBOOKING/LAPBOOK Alert

Add 1563 Liborum Prohibitorum to your Protestant Reformation timeline.

DID YOU KNOW?
The Roman Inquisition was not as violent (nor as long) as the Spanish Inquisition that was taking place over in Spain. The Roman Inquisition was a group mainly in Rome that primarily sought out heretics and tried to convert them or get them to recant. Some people were excommunicated, others were placed under house arrest, and still others were handed over to the authorities. In fact the 300 Protestants who were burned at the stake during Bloody Mary's reign were executed by *her* command—not by the command of the Church (though the Church was the one who questioned the heretics and handed them over to the queen). The Spanish Inquisition was much more bloody; people were tortured in attempts to convert them, and execution was much more common. In the year 2000, the pope apologized for the things the Catholic Church had done during the Inquisition.

NATIONAL LIBRARY OF ST. MARKS IN VENICE, ITALY

NOTABLE ARCHITECTURE

At the same time all these meetings were being held, a beautiful building was being designed over in Venice, Italy. The Marciana Library (also known as the Library of Saint Mark) was originally started in 1537 and mostly completed in 1564 (though more work was done over the next 19 years); it is a beautiful example of classic architecture. The designer used large columns, carvings, and sculptures as well as classic arches on the outside of the building, which made up part of Saint Mark's Square. The main floor was designed to hold books, while the upstairs had an ornately decorated reading room with the walls and arched ceilings covered in paintings. Desks were set up for scholars to come and research. However this wasn't the first home for the library. It had existed in various churches and even the Doges' *(dohj-es)* Palace before it was made into a building all on its own. Its construction was not without its difficulties. At one point part of the library collapsed because the structure could not bear its own weight. The books were eventually moved to their new home, but it would be many years before the final arches were finished. Despite the hiccups, the library still stands today in Venice—a remarkable memento to the Renaissance era.

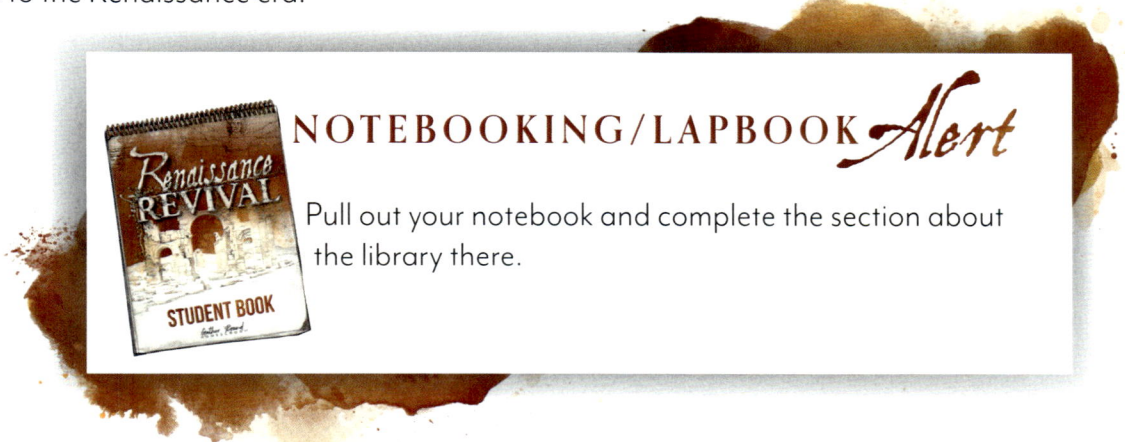

NOTEBOOKING/LAPBOOK *Alert*

Pull out your notebook and complete the section about the library there.

DID YOU KNOW? Venice, Italy, was originally a group of islands along a lagoon and surrounded by shallow, marshy waters. During the Middle Ages, Lombard invaders forced many Italians to flee to the area, and the need for a city arose. It was built on hundreds of islands, and the natural waterways were used to travel between the different areas. Quickly the citizens realized that they needed to **fortify** these passages, and so they dug trenches and built them up. They also constructed their houses on wood pilings that were under the water. While Venice is known as the "floating city," it is actually more accurately a "sinking city" as it sinks a little more each year, making it susceptible to flooding. Check out some videos on the resources page in the app to see why it is such a popular tourist destination today!

CONGO REVIVAL

In 1953, missionaries in the Belgian Congo were longing for a move of God. Work was being done, and people were being saved, but it felt like the wind had gone out of their sails. There was no passion—people still went about sinning, and a remnant was dissatisfied. As a result the missionaries decided to gather and pray once a month for revival, reading stories of other revivals to stir up their hunger. During one regularly-scheduled conference, a prayer meeting was happening. The missionaries were gathered in their home while the locals were meeting at the school. All of a sudden, the missionaries' prayer time was interrupted by sounds of loud crying from the school. They ran to make sure that everyone was okay and ran headlong into . . . revival. Many people were crying and asking God for forgiveness as they confessed their sins, while others were lying on the ground like the priests in 2 Chronicles 5:13–14 who couldn't stand in the glory of God. As the time grew late, the missionaries attempted to close the meeting, but they were unsuccessful because the Spirit moved for 24 hours. The missionaries excitedly told the outlying stations about what had happened, and expectation arose everywhere for God to move . . . and move He did.

When some of the wives began to shake when touched by the power of God, it made many people uncomfortable until one of the leaders had a vision of the congregation shaking and confessing their sins, leading him to say, "It is one thing to pray for revival, quite another to be willing for it."[14] Like we learned in previous lessons, the Holy Spirit moves in mysterious ways. One night the men and women decided to separate so they could be more open to confessing their sins. The men were hit first, and the women got up to find out what was going on. When they saw what was happening, they went back to continue praying, and the Holy Spirit fell upon them as well. One man was unsettled by what was happening and left, but after only five steps, his legs seemed to be stuck, and he could go no further until he got right with God. Many things happened during this time—buildings were shaken, and one meeting was filled with the sound of a hurricane, even though there were no clouds, and the trees weren't moving outside. Just like during the first Pentecost in the book of Acts, the Spirit fell with incredible power for two years in the Congo region. The churches grew both in numbers and in passion, and the nation would never be the same.

EXTENSION ACTIVITY

Check out the video on the resources page in the app to hear a firsthand account of the Congo Revival!

HANDS-ON *Activity*

Venice is famous for its canals and waterways; many tourists go on sightseeing or romantic boat tours through the labyrinth that only the locals understand. Design your own maze that you have to navigate through like an obstacle course. Then take your family on a tour through the passageway!

VOCABULARY

EARLY READER
assembly: *a gathering of people*
fortify: *to strengthen*

EARLY ELEMENTARY
fortify: *to strengthen*
edict: *an official order made by someone with authority*

UPPER ELEMENTARY
edict: *an official order made by someone with authority*
pervade: *to spread through and take over*

MIDDLE SCHOOL
pervade: *to spread through and take over*
refute: *to prove that something is wrong*

HIGH SCHOOL
refute: *to prove that something is wrong*
recant: *to take back what was said*

Renaissance and REVIVAL

LESSON 16: GIORGIO VASARI

The history books we read are full of stories about important people who did important things—kind of like the main characters in a play or movie. But just as crucial are the ones who record the stories. These people are known as *chroniclers*. In fact this is where the name for the book of Chronicles in the Bible comes from: it's a written historical account of what happened. Chroniclers recognized the significance of their time and wrote down everything they could—sometimes traveling to conduct interviews and gather firsthand testimonies from those who had lived through the events they were recording. If no one had written them down, the stories would have been regarded as nothing more than **myths** with no conclusive evidence. Instead we have many accounts from different people, allowing us to put them together like puzzle pieces to **corroborate** the stories that have been told. It seems that writing is important after all! Today we're going to learn about one man who played the role of both the character and the playwright . . . Giorgio Vasari.

THE LIFE AND TIMES OF VASARI

Born in Arezzo, Italy, in 1511, Vasari grew up during the glory of the Italian Renaissance. He was raised among the greats like Michelangelo during the time of Catherine de' Medici, Henry VIII, and even Queen Mary I. Like many Italian boys his age, Vasari went to school in Florence, where he studied art in the Medici schools. When he was old enough, he began taking commissions from the Medici family, even painting a portrait of Lorenzo the Magnificent (who had died many years earlier). He produced various forms of artwork such as oil paintings and frescoes. In fact, one of his most famous works is a series of frescoes based on the life of Pope Paul III (the very same one who organized the Council of Trent) that he was said to have painted in 100 days. It was commissioned by the pope's grandson and namesake, Alessandro Farnese. A common rumor is that Vasari was showing Michelangelo the paintings, proudly explaining how quickly he had completed them, and the elder master sculptor responded with a cutting, "It shows."[15] Other sources say that Michelangelo was a mentor and friend to the younger Vasari, making the legend less likely. What do you think?

GIORGIO VASARI

TEACHER'S GUIDE LESSON 16   84   GIORGIO VASARI

> **NOTEBOOKING/LAPBOOK Alert**
>
> Pull out your timeline figures. Place the cutout for Giorgio Vasari in the correct spot to show his place in history as well as how he fits into the story. Then complete the section on Vasari in your student notebook.

Painting came easily to Vasari, and he took on many different commissions to help pay the bills—though his real skill would come in another form . . . architecture. It's important to remember that there wasn't necessarily a school for architecture during this time. Often artists who had an eye for beauty and form would dabble in this area, and some were better at it than others. Vasari made some mistakes as he branched into this new field, but he worked on many buildings that still stand today, including the Uffizi Gallery (a museum) and Piazza dei Cavalieri (an education center). His largest undertaking, the Vasari Corridor, was named after him. This covered walkway is found in Florence and connects various buildings—even crossing the river. It is .5 miles (750 m) long and was built in only five months, which is pretty incredible considering its length. Government officials were able to use it to walk quickly between buildings without being seen or **accosted** by the public. It included a hall where people could gather for larger meetings, and the walls were decorated with frescoes of the Medici family. It was a unique structure at the time and a functional one too. The corridor remains almost perfectly preserved today, and visitors can view various art pieces as they tour the walkway (if they make a reservation that is).

> **NOTEBOOKING/LAPBOOK Alert**
>
> Pull out your student notebook and complete the section on the Vasari Corridor. If you are using our lapbook add-on, assemble the Vasari Corridor booklet.

VASARI'S CHRONICLES

A **prolific** and highly successful artist and architect, Vasari had no shortage of skill. But his most impactful contribution to the Renaissance was actually not his building plans or paintings but rather his book, *Lives of the Most Eminent Painters, Sculptors, and Architects*. Recognizing that it wasn't just the masterpieces that needed to be remembered but also the artists behind them, he began chronicling the stories of the great men and women of the Renaissance. The book, dedicated to Cosimo I de' Medici, is like an encyclopedia of sorts that includes portraits and biographies of the ordinary people behind the chisels and paintbrushes of various artworks. As a chronicler, Vasari wasn't very consistent, and there are many instances of dates not lining up. But still to this day, his book remains one of the most primary sources of the Renaissance, giving us a glimpse that we might never have had if he had not put pen to paper.

THE JESUS MOVEMENT

The 1960s was a **tumultuous** time. The world was full of problems: the Cuban Missile Crisis, the Vietnam War, the Arab-Israeli War, racial tensions, and assassinations of beloved leaders such as President Kennedy and Martin Luther King Jr. meant that there was never a dull moment—and everyone had an opinion about everything. A group of mostly young people—affectionately remembered as *hippies*—rejected it all. They stood against the fighting that was going on and were known to burn the draft cards that required them to go to war. In fact this group often protested any form of control or government. They usually lived together in communes, tents, or houses; traveled in Volkswagen buses; and had a certain look: bare feet and long hair (including beards). The women also often had flowers woven into their braids. Hippies wore shirts and carried signs with the slogan "Make Love, Not War," a saying that kind of summed up their main values. It was all about doing what made you happy, whether that meant drinking, doing drugs, dabbling in the New Age movement or the occult, or finding love in the arms of another. At the root of it all was actually a deep emptiness—a generation that was tired of all the violence and hate and seeking the world's answers for whatever was the opposite of that. But the world could not fill the void, which was a reality that would shake an entire generation during the Jesus Movement.

It all began in California with a few hippies who had been recently converted. They opened up a coffeehouse in 1967 called The Living Room. They also created a home, which they dubbed the House of Acts, where new converts could come and be discipled. One of these converts was 19-year-old Lonnie Frisbee, a man who would eventually travel around and speak to his generation in a big way. He partnered with a church called Calvary Chapel and held gatherings that led to its **rapid** growth. He also opened up many more homes where people could live together and be discipled, including one named the House of Miracles. This revival was called a *movement* for a reason. It was a generation lost that only the same generation could call back. Instead of trying to convert people with control and threats of hell, leaders led people to Jesus through kindness and love—the very things that they were searching for. Hundreds of communal homes were set up all across the United States, where people could stay and grow in their faith. Large rallies were held, but this time, instead of empty words and promises, they were filled with the hope of the Gospel—and people came in droves. The new converts were called Jesus Freaks by their peers, a label they accepted as an honor.

What about the telltale spark of every revival: prayer? This is truly what makes this movement unique. There was no one great speaker. There isn't a story of two little old ladies who were burdened to pray for more. But you can be assured that concerned parents and grandparents everywhere were on their knees asking God to bring their prodigals home. Just like the missionary in the Congo who said, "It is one thing to pray for revival, quite another to be willing for it,"[16] this revival wasn't an easy pill to swallow. Hippies who had been converted still often dressed and talked the same way. They liked the same styles of music, and they challenged religion in general when they walked into churches in their bare feet, swaying to the music and holding nothing back. Like we have read in Isaiah 43:19, God brought revival, and He did it in an entirely new way that the world probably wasn't expecting. Many rejected the movement; however, for those who would embrace it . . . a great harvest was waiting. No one knows for certain the exact number, but it is estimated that over 2 million people gave their lives to Jesus in the USA alone! Many young people left their old ways behind and stepped into their new callings on the mission field as either evangelists or pastors. It's amazing what can happen in a coffeehouse, isn't it?

HANDS-ON *Activity*

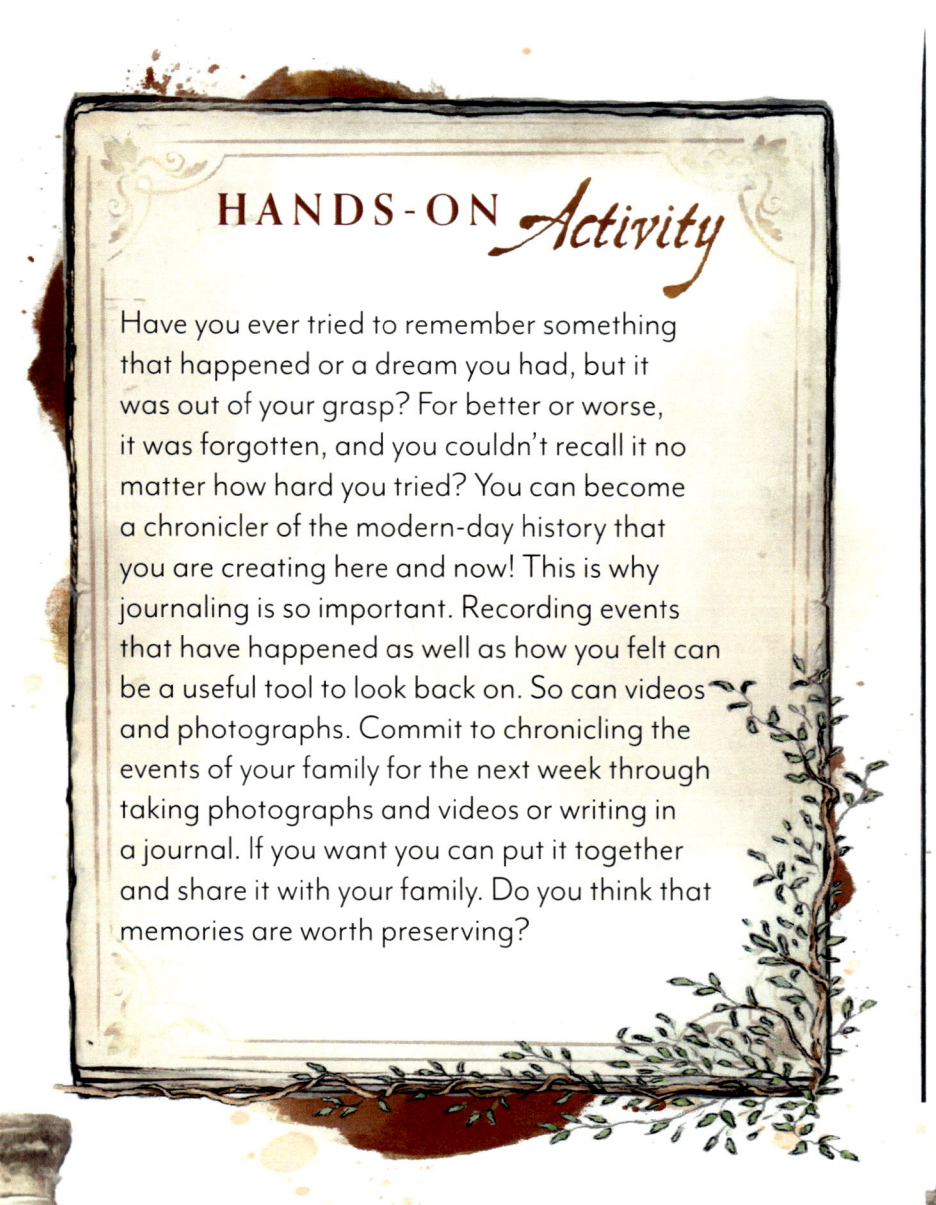

Have you ever tried to remember something that happened or a dream you had, but it was out of your grasp? For better or worse, it was forgotten, and you couldn't recall it no matter how hard you tried? You can become a chronicler of the modern-day history that you are creating here and now! This is why journaling is so important. Recording events that have happened as well as how you felt can be a useful tool to look back on. So can videos and photographs. Commit to chronicling the events of your family for the next week through taking photographs and videos or writing in a journal. If you want you can put it together and share it with your family. Do you think that memories are worth preserving?

VOCABULARY

EARLY READER
rapid: *very fast*
myth: *a made-up story*

EARLY ELEMENTARY
myth: *a made-up story*
prolific: *producing a great amount of something*

UPPER ELEMENTARY
prolific: *producing a great amount of something*
tumultuous: *full of upheaval and chaos*

MIDDLE SCHOOL
tumultuous: *full of upheaval and chaos*
corroborate: *to prove with evidence that something is true*

HIGH SCHOOL
corroborate: *to prove with evidence that something is true*
accost: *to approach someone and talk to them in an aggressive way*

Renaissance and Revival

LESSON 17: WILLIAM SHAKESPEARE

We've talked about Shakespeare's work a lot in your student pages, but today we get to peel back the curtain and learn a bit more about the man himself. The sad reality is that, while the literature he produced survived, there was no chronicler who wrote about who he was as a person. As a result, many things about him are left to **speculation**. We don't know his birthday or much about his personality other than what we can surmise from his writings—in fact there's a whole list of things that we don't have the answers to. But from what we do know, a picture can be painted of an extraordinary yet ordinary person who would forever influence not just the world of literature but the English language as a whole. Grab yourself a cup of tea and let's **delve** into the world of poetry, scripts, and plays as we follow the breadcrumbs of Shakespeare's life.

EARLY LIFE

No one knows for certain the exact day of William Shakespeare's birth, as there is no public or written record of it. The first time his name pops up in any documents is for his baptism. During this time in history (and in some churches still today), babies were baptized as soon as possible, usually within a week or less of being born. And so the date just three days before his baptism—April 23, 1564—was chosen to remember and celebrate the birthday of William Shakespeare. Ironically he would die on this very same day 52 years later—a date that we *do* have a record of—though his actual cause of death remains a mystery. What we do know is that Shakespeare was born in England. His father was a glover; he would buy leather hides and tan them in the backyard, making them soft and **supple** before cutting them and distributing them to women who would sew them into gloves for him to sell. There are records of Shakespeare's father getting involved in politics, buying and selling goods as a merchant, and even lending out money. The family did well for themselves. They weren't nobles and didn't have extreme wealth, but they did much better than most other families of the time. Shakespeare's parents had eight children, though many of them would not survive through childhood (as was common during that period). William was thought to have had a happy, normal childhood, learning Latin and grammar at school and being a fairly ordinary boy. The reality is, though, that no one knows for certain what he did or what he was like, as there are no records of him during this time of his life.

NOTEBOOKING/LAPBOOK *Alert*

Place the figure for Shakespeare on your timeline to show how he fit into the Renaissance.

TEACHER'S GUIDE LESSON 17

ADULT LIFE

When he was only 18 years old, Shakespeare married Anne Hathaway, a woman who was 26 and therefore quite a bit older than him. For a while the young couple focused on building a family, raising two girls and one boy. No one knows for certain how Shakespeare got into writing, but when all of the theaters were closed because of the bubonic plague, his first works began to appear. He started out with writing poetry before moving on to **sonnets** and plays. He also created a special society called the Lord Chamberlain's Men (later called the King's Men), where he served as both a playwright (someone who writes plays) and an actor. He wrote his scripts in a unique style called *iambic pentameter*, which allowed them to be read with a rhythm, making them easier to memorize. This meant that as fast as Shakespeare could write, his plays could be practiced and performed. He had a group of actors ready at his disposal and was familiar with everything needed to produce a play. When the plague passed, plays were put on throughout London and even in the king's court—in fact this is where the group's new name came from. There were only a few acting societies that had permission to perform in the city, and when the theater was forced to close down because the lease ran out, Shakespeare decided to do something **drastic** . . . build his own theater.

PORTRAIT OF WILLIAM SHAKESPEARE

NOTEBOOKING/LAPBOOK Alert

Complete the activity on William Shakespeare in your student book or lapbook!

Shakespeare's theater—called The Globe—was a round open-air amphitheater that had seats most of the way around it (except for where the stage was). There was even an open place near the stage where people could stand to watch, and the entire building could hold an estimated 3,000 spectators. Constructing this theater was costly and required a number of investors—including Shakespeare, himself, as well as some of the other actors, all of whom contributed a chunk of the funds out of their personal coffers. The Globe was constructed as quickly as possible for the first performance of Shakespeare's new tragedy, *Julius Caesar*. His plays did so well that when the previous **venue** became available again, it was used along with the new theater—one for the summer months and the other during the winter. However, one tragic night a fire burned the Globe down in just an hour. While it wasn't necessary, the troupe decided to rebuild the theater even better than before, proof of just how popular it was at the time and how successful the plays were. The group changed the world of acting forever, and Shakespeare's plays would remain as some of the most profound works of the Late Renaissance era, having a lasting impact on the English language as a whole.

TEACHER'S GUIDE LESSON 17 — **WILLIAM SHAKESPEARE**

> **DID YOU KNOW?** During this time in history, it was considered inappropriate for women to act in plays. Most of the female roles were actually played by men who would wear wigs and dresses, put on heavy makeup, and talk in high-pitched voices. This didn't mean that women did not perform at all, however. In other arenas they were known to sing, dance, and even tumble through the air in circus-like acrobatics for entertainment. What do you think? Should women have been allowed to act on stage?

TIMOR REVIVAL

From 1965 to 1970—around the same time as the Jesus Movement—something amazing was happening over in Indonesia. While many natives on the island of Timor had heard about Jesus and went to church, they also owned amulets and charms or consulted shamans for luck or healing. In fact some pastors believed that they, themselves, had supernatural, magical abilities that made them more powerful—and this attracted needy people to their churches. But all of that would change when multiple people had visions that led them to start a prayer group, asking the Lord for revival in their church (the Maranatha Church). Their prayers seemed to stir up a hunger, and it wasn't long before people began burning their amulets and charms and wholly dedicating themselves to the Lord. When one young girl (called Priscilla) preached to her generation, many youth gave their lives to Jesus. There was no doubt about it: something was happening!

One Sunday night 200 people joined in prayer, and the Holy Spirit came in power—like the day of Pentecost in the book of Acts. Many heard a loud wind, and the fire brigade was called because the community saw flames. When the brigade arrived at the church, it discovered that the flames were not actually burning anything up—it was kind of like the burning bush that Moses encountered![17] The community members that had come to help put out the fire were struck by the power of God, and many of them started following Jesus that same day. This very church—the epicenter of the revival—would send out teams all over the island to share the gospel. The power of God moved across the people with signs and wonders just like in the book of Acts in the Bible. There were stories of pretty much every type of miracle: water being turned into wine, people speaking in unknown languages, and the sick being healed of diseases or even raised from the dead. People had prophecies and visions, and even storms were calmed so others might believe. The communities were deeply impacted—stolen property was returned, crime went down, fighting decreased, and the churches grew in great numbers and sent out missionaries to many other regions. When reports of these wonders reached America, not everyone was excited about it. Some groups (referred to as *cessationists*), believed the gifts of the Spirit had ceased in the New Testament and that these miracles were heretical. Two men with these beliefs decided to go to the island to write a book against the movement. They aimed to discredit the miracles that had occurred, which led to many people in the West to question the move of God. A reporter was sent by Tyndale House Publishers to get to the bottom of things, and after talking to many people who had been healed or touched, the reporter was convinced that the miraculous stories had not been embellished. Were people lying, or did God truly pour out His Spirit? What do you think?

HANDS-ON *Activity*

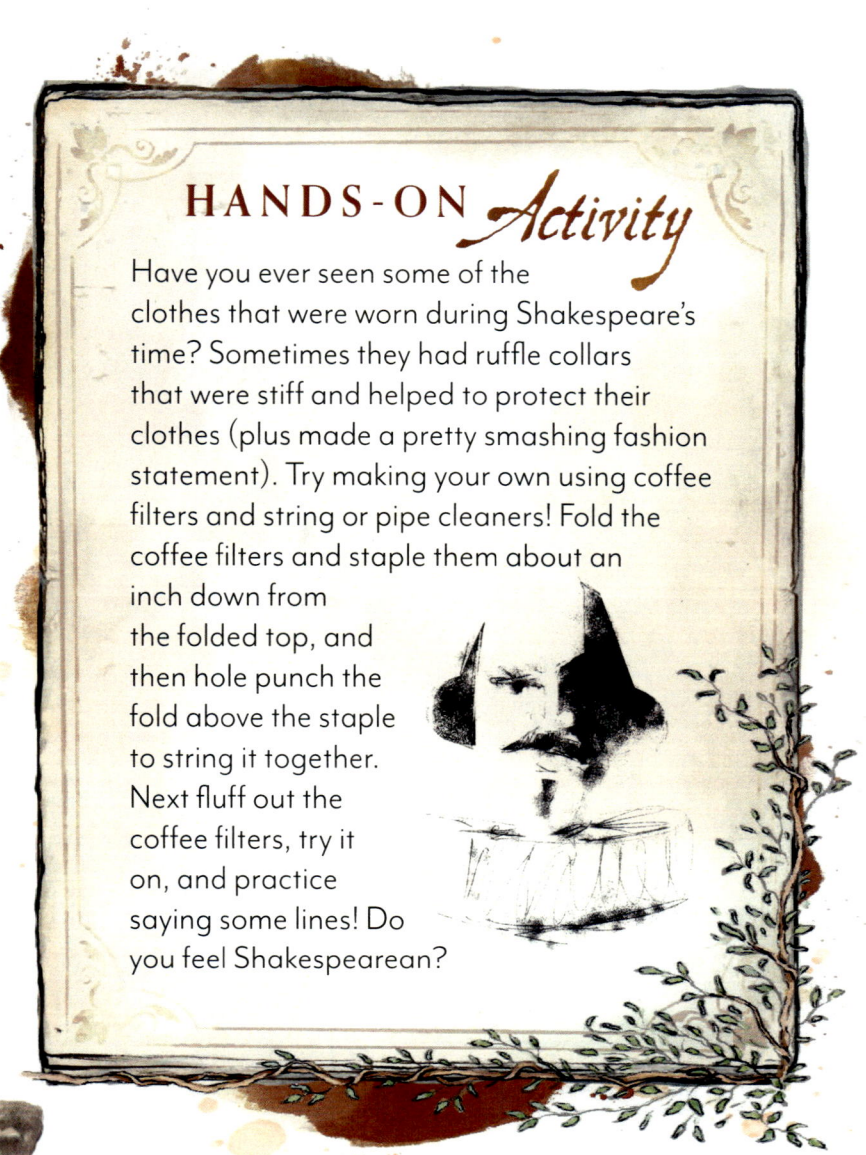

Have you ever seen some of the clothes that were worn during Shakespeare's time? Sometimes they had ruffle collars that were stiff and helped to protect their clothes (plus made a pretty smashing fashion statement). Try making your own using coffee filters and string or pipe cleaners! Fold the coffee filters and staple them about an inch down from the folded top, and then hole punch the fold above the staple to string it together. Next fluff out the coffee filters, try it on, and practice saying some lines! Do you feel Shakespearean?

VOCABULARY

EARLY READER
sonnet: *a poem*
venue: *the location where an event takes place*

EARLY ELEMENTARY
venue: *the location where an event takes place*
drastic: *extreme and sudden*

UPPER ELEMENTARY
drastic: *extreme and sudden*
speculation: *a guess about something*

MIDDLE SCHOOL
speculation: *a guess about something*
delve: *to examine something closely in order to get more information*

HIGH SCHOOL
delve: *to examine something closely in order to get more information*
supple: *able to move easily*

Renaissance and Revival

LESSON 18: GALILEO

Who was born in the same year as Shakespeare, spent over eight years locked in his home on house arrest, was a college dropout, had three children but was never married, and has a finger on display at a museum in Italy? It's one of the most famous scientists and mathematicians of all time . . . Galileo Galilei. Galileo had a pretty adventurous life that was marked by curiosity and wonder—traits that would eventually get him into trouble. He was a dedicated Catholic, and his faith was a driving force behind his studies. Like many of our other Renaissance figures, he was not appreciated in his time and paid a great price for the contributions that he made to his field. However, today—centuries after he died—he is regarded as the "father of modern astronomy," and NASA has even named a spacecraft after him! Galileo might not have lived to see the fruits of his labor, but his impact on the world was no small matter. Let's unravel the scroll of his life to see where the ripples of his work all began.

THINK ABOUT IT The idea of being famous is a big draw for many people. That's because each one of us has a desire to do something that matters—to be known and recognized or appreciated. But the true movers and shakers of history were often rejected in their own times, only becoming household names many years after their deaths. Which would you prefer: to be famous during your lifetime or to be remembered long after you are gone? The reality is, as Christians, our earthly **legacy** (our good name) is not the most important thing. The Bible teaches us to lay up treasures for ourselves in heaven; we do this by living a life that honors God and by drawing close to Jesus. Like Peter getting out of the boat,[18] we keep our eyes fixed on what is eternal (Jesus) instead of what is temporary (people's opinions of us). Do you think that you treasure the applause of your peers over the "well done" of the Father? Talk about it as a family.

TEACHER'S GUIDE LESSON 18

THE LIFE OF A SCHOLAR

Galileo was born on February 15, 1564, in Pisa, Italy. His father was a musician and scholar, and his mother was from an aristocratic family. While they weren't particularly wealthy, Galileo was raised comfortably along with his five siblings and was provided with a good education as well as opportunities to **excel**. Galileo's father wanted him to pursue a career in medicine, so the 16-year-old was sent to the University of Pisa. But the young man found himself far more fascinated by mathematics and philosophy instead and ended up dropping out of school to pursue his own studies (kind of like being homeschooled but by yourself). During this time he conducted many experiments relating to motion and gravity, which were later expanded upon by physicists like Sir Isaac Newton. Despite the fact that he didn't complete a degree, Galileo's studies were effective, and by the time he was 25, he was teaching at the very school he had previously left.

As a young adult, Galileo never married, but he did have three children with a woman who was beneath his station and therefore not considered a suitable match. The **unconventional** family lived together for a time until Galileo moved to Florence. Some people mistakenly believe that he invented the telescope, but the instrument was already in use in the Netherlands when he got his hands on it—though originally it was only used for surveying long distances on land. Galileo improved upon its design and was among the first to point it to the heavens, observing stars and planets through the small eyepiece. While Copernicus had made his observations with the naked eye, Galileo had a closer view, and he was credited with discovering that Saturn had rings (though he couldn't see clear enough to tell what they were), that Jupiter had four moons, and that the moon had craters and mountains. In the beginning he worked with the Catholic church, getting special permission to study Copernicus' works as long as he didn't support the man's views. But his study of the sky led him to be more and more convinced that the Earth was indeed moving around the sun, and he started advocating for Copernicus' theory. These beliefs got his own publications placed on the Index of Prohibited Books, and Galileo was ordered to Rome where he was placed under trial by the Inquisition. Some sources say that he apologized, while others claim that he defended himself. Regardless of what happened, he was sentenced to house arrest, where he spent the remainder of his life. At the ripe old age of 70, Galileo was considered an old man in an era when many did not live past their forties. With all the time in the world, he wrote one final book, which was smuggled out by **accomplices** to be printed in Holland. He finally died of sickness all alone when he was 77 years old.

PORTRAIT OF GALILEO GALILEI BY JUSTUS SUSTERMANS

NOTEBOOKING/LAPBOOK Alert

Pull out your timeline and place the figure for Galileo Galilei on it. Then complete the activity to show what you learned about him!

TEACHER'S GUIDE LESSON 18 GALILEO

REVIVAL IN SOUTH AMERICA

When a young 19-year-old man from Bolivia named Julio Ruibal traveled to America to go to medical school, he wasn't expecting to encounter Jesus. Despite being heavily involved in the occult, he attended a meeting—and it was here that he **irrevocably** gave his life to Jesus. He went back to the gathering a second night where he found thousands of people locked out of the event because it was full. The newly-saved college student stood up among the crowd and began telling his testimony and praying for the disappointed masses—and God showed up. Despite missing the headline speaker, many left healed of their ailments, and this young man was filled with faith for what God could do. After a time Julio dropped out of school, realizing he was called to bring healing not as a doctor but as an evangelist instead. No one could have anticipated the impact that this young man (who received the nickname Apostle of the Andes) would have all across South America.

When Julio returned home, he began sharing the gospel with his friends, family, and community. Small Bible studies turned into larger ones until the gatherings had to be split into multiple homes. God performed many signs and wonders through the prayers of Julio and his friends as they ministered—including healing, food being multiplied, demons being cast out, water being turned into wine for Communion, and dreams and visions. The entire city began to talk about what God was doing in the hiddenness of these home meetings, and Julio felt that God was leading him and the others to hold larger gatherings for the masses—though the young men didn't know how they could possibly afford such a thing. When traditional fundraising didn't work, the group chose to surrender to God's way instead, not realizing that the Lord had a plan that was far better than theirs. Meanwhile a paralyzed man (who Julio did not know held a prominent position in the government) was healed and began to walk—not an uncommon thing to happen when the new believers prayed for people. A short time later, the president of Bolivia arrived, amazed at what had happened to this man that he worked with. Julio prayed with him and his wife, leading them to Jesus. They then asked how they could help. From that moment on, the nation's stadiums were at Julio's disposal. The events held there were heavily advertised, and Julio was even offered the president's personal jet to allow him to travel wherever the Lord would lead! With backing and money, he began to preach to tens of thousands of people at a time, during which multitudes would pile their walkers, wheelchairs, and crutches on the stage and walk out on healed legs or with renewed spines.

JULIO RUIBAL

After Julio got married and started a family, he felt called to continue his ministry work together with his wife and two small daughters in Cali, Colombia. Here a group named the 1,000 Trumpets began to meet and pray for God to change Colombia, the most violent nation in the world. The movement started and swelled with prayer. Stadiums were rented out not for preaching but for quarterly all-night prayer **vigils**. After these incredible prayer events, thousands of people were saved, and violence in the region began to go down for the first time in decades. Yet at what seemed the height of revival, in 1995 Julio was shot on the street and died. This tragedy could have destroyed everything—the enemy surely hoped that it would—but we serve a God who can redeem even the darkest trials, and instead, Julio's death brought one of the greatest miracles. Over 200 churches signed a covenant of unity, deciding to work with one another rather than focusing on building their own followings, and revival burst forth like streams of living water. When asked about their strategy later on, some of the leaders were known to have said, "We don't have time to plan. We're too busy pulling the nets into the boat."[19] The city of Cali was forever changed, and it is estimated that hundreds of thousands of people were saved because of the simple obedience of a bunch of young people who said yes to Jesus.

HANDS-ON Activity

Galileo is known for a lot of different things because he was good at a lot of things! Long before Sir Isaac Newton "discovered" gravity, Galileo conducted studies about the downward force on objects. He also came up with some ways to test his ideas that would contribute to the scientific method we use today. Try conducting your own gravity experiment by dropping two objects from the same height. Do you think one will fall faster than the other? Go through the steps of the scientific method to find out.

VOCABULARY

EARLY READER
excel: *to stand out or do something better than others*
legacy: *something that gets passed onto future generations*

EARLY ELEMENTARY
legacy: *something that gets passed onto future generations*
vigil: *an event where people stay up in order to support someone or something through prayer*

UPPER ELEMENTARY
vigil: *an event where people stay up in order to support someone or something through prayer*
unconventional: *outside of what's normally accepted by culture*

MIDDLE SCHOOL
unconventional: *outside of what's normally accepted by culture*
accomplice: *a person who helps someone else break the law*

HIGH SCHOOL
accomplice: *a person who helps someone else break the law*
irrevocable: *not able to be changed or taken back*

Renaissance and Revival

LESSON 19: KING JAMES

Can you imagine what it would be like to become king at only a year old? Picture a royal cradle, royal attendants, royal advisors, royal diaper changes—maybe even a royal pacifier! While children have certainly inherited thrones throughout history, they usually don't have it happen when they are so young. As you'll soon discover, however, our final monarch had a pretty extraordinary story. It might sound like a reel on social media playing over and over again, but like so many of the other people we have studied, this king was not particularly liked during his time on the stage of history. Despite that, he remains one of the most famous figures of all time—mainly because of the Bible that was named after him: the King James Version (or KJV). What led to this translation being named after a king? Let's find out!

EARLY LIFE

James Charles Stuart was born in Scotland on June 19, 1566. When his mother (Mary, Queen of Scots) was imprisoned, she was forced to name her only son as her **successor**, though he was only 13 months old at the time. For most of his childhood, the young king was passed around from noble to noble, each hoping to influence him for their own gains. He was tutored in a wide range of subjects, but his most critical schooling was learning how to navigate the political scene of his own court. By the time he was in his teens, James was said to have been a **shrewd** politician, well-equipped to read between the lines of not only what was said but also what wasn't. The regents who ruled in his stead had some troubles of their own, each leaning toward their own biases and ultimately paying the price. The final regent (whose name was also James) was a supporter of the young king—which was a dangerous political position considering others wanted his mother, Mary, to lead the country toward Catholicism instead. When the regent was found guilty of being a part of the plot to murder Queen Mary's husband, he was executed for treason and the young king began to rule in his own right when he was only a young teenager. Being so young, he decided to bring in his own advisors, including his Catholic cousin who he had a very close (some say too close) relationship with. Some of the Protestant nobles did not approve and banished his cousin, seeing King James as a threat.

To seize control, some nobles plotted to kidnap King James, keeping him locked away for about a year. He finally escaped, sentencing the main conspirator to death. In the world of royals, kidnapping was a very real threat—but it was even more risky for those involved in the plot should they be unsuccessful. After escaping from his prison and sentencing the main conspirator of the plot to death. As he had learned, the religious war was dangerous, and one wrong step could prove deadly. One thing his caretakers had done quite well was to turn the young ruler against his Catholic mother and raise him to be Protestant instead. When it was discovered that Mary was **conspiring** against her cousin in England to try and take the throne, she was convicted of treason and sentenced to death. James was faced with a choice: support a mother that he never really knew and risk displeasing his subjects as well as the queen of England, or play the political game. He made a mild protest (which was more of a formality than anything) and then washed his hands of his mother once and for all.

NOTEBOOKING/LAPBOOK Alert
Cut out your timeline figure for King James VI (also known as King James I) and place it on your timeline.

ADULT LIFE

With the drama of kidnappings and conspiracies behind him (at least for now), the king arranged a marriage with a Danish princess named Anne, who was only 14 at the time. Together they ruled Scotland and raised a family. Meanwhile over in England, Queen Elizabeth died, leaving no heir to take the throne. When no one was found to be suitable, the court decided to crown King James VI of Scotland as King James I of England. This was basically the birth of Great Britain—though it wouldn't truly be named that nor be fully unified until later. The king was thrilled; he packed up his family and moved to his new country, promising to return to Scotland and check on things over the years. But it did not go as well for James in England as it had in Scotland. The new king offended the parliament and eventually dissolved it. He went against the public opinion and imposed new taxes to help pay for his luxurious lifestyle. He and Anne were big supporters of the arts—in fact it was in England that they first saw the King's Men perform and also became acquainted with Shakespeare. The couple loved the parties and adventure that London had to offer, so the king would end up only returning to his homeland one time over the next 22 years. With his hands full in England, his subjects in Scotland were left primarily to their own devices, and slowly but surely he lost much of his control of a land that he had largely washed his hands of (at least in its citizens' minds), just as he had done with his mother.

KING JAMES I OF ENGLAND AND VI OF SCOTLAND BY JOHN DE CRITZ THE ELDER

DID YOU KNOW? Have you ever known someone who had the same name as their father? To help it be less confusing, it is not uncommon for families to give their children nicknames or to shorten their names so everyone knows who they are talking about. The government can get confused by it, too, which is why it is important for parents to use the suffix *junior* (Jr.) or *senior* (Sr.) in legal documents. The same thing happened throughout history with those who only used their first names, like popes and kings. To clarify who these people were, they were given a number behind their names to show what order they came in and how they fit into the history books. Do you think doing this sounds more regal? Try saying your name and adding "the first" after it to hear what it sounds like!

SUSPICIONS AND FEARS

King James was known to be a **suspicious** individual—and that wasn't without good reason. From his kidnapping and the brutal political games of court to rumors of witchcraft directed at his family and conspiracies all around . . . royal life was **perilous**. Take a look at some of the events below and judge for yourself.

1582: The 16-year-old king was kidnapped and held hostage for a year.

1589: Queen Anne went to meet her new husband, but her boat was **assailed** by storms, and she was forced to wait in Norway. The blame was placed on witches who were said to have sent a contrary wind. This was a great concern to the king and led him to write about the dangers of witchcraft in a book, *Daemonologie*, which explained how to identify and punish a witch. His passion for rooting out this evil led to many witch hunts in Scotland and resulted in thousands of women being executed.

1605: The Gunpowder Plot was discovered—a plan to assassinate the king and queen and place their nine-year-old daughter, Elizabeth, on the throne as a puppet queen (who could be raised Catholic). A cellar underneath Parliament was rented out and filled with barrels of gunpowder and firewood. When a servant tipped off his master, telling him not to attend meetings the next day, it led to the arrest of Guy Fawkes, who was caught with evidence in hand. He later confessed and was executed for high treason.

These rumors, stories, and events made the king incredibly distrustful—some would even say that he became fearful. While he had been somewhat successful in Scotland at managing things, it appeared to be a losing battle in England. James' attempts to join together the kingdoms of Scotland and England were opposed by both nations, which wanted to maintain their freedoms and identities. He even designed the first Union Jack flag by combining the crosses of the two countries. He declared himself the king of Great Britain, a name that neither country was particularly fond of. Meanwhile the religious war was becoming more and more convoluted as different denominations (such as Calvinism, Presbyterian, Anglican, and Lutheran) rose up, each with their own ideas. To help unite the Church of England, the king authorized a new English translation of the Bible. For a time it was referred to as the King James Authorized Bible, but its name was eventually shortened to the King James Version. The translation was actually already mostly done by William Tyndale (remember him?), and over 80 percent of it is actually in his words. The scholars who were commissioned to finish the work took seven years to match the style of Tyndale and complete the New Testament. In the end James was not considered a highly successful king in England, but he is still well known today because of the Bible that bears his name.

BROWNSVILLE REVIVAL

In 1992 a Korean minister prophesied that a revival would come to Pensacola, Florida, and spread across America. This was not a new prophecy, as a number of others had said the same thing over the past decade. When Pastor John Kilpatrick of the Brownsville Assembly of God heard of the prophecy, he was stirred with a hunger to see it come to pass, and he began to focus his church on prayer. Together the congregation decided to cancel their normal Sunday evening worship services and hold prayer meetings instead. This extraordinary prayer went on for nearly three years, and the whole time the church was faithful to intercede for their city and nation. In 1995 Pastor John asked evangelist Steve Hill to come and preach for their Father's Day service. John had just lost his mother and needed a break. Mr. Hill preached both the morning and evening services, calling forward those who needed prayer—and 1,000 people rushed to the stage. The gathering was extended and continued until 4:00 p.m., allowing for only a short break before an evening service that lasted well into the night. There was no question that God was moving, and Hill was there for it. He canceled all of his other engagements and moved his family to Pensacola in preparation for what God was going to do there.

Over the next five years, the Holy Spirit was poured out in a powerful way. The Brownsville Revival was marked by a tangible awareness of the presence of God and resulted in salvations and repentance. One 14-year-old girl named Charity James sang a song called "Mercy Seat" for the altar calls, during which thousands of people would come to the front to surrender their lives and hearts to Jesus. Many new songs were written in these five years. As a new sound came forth, God's presence filled the room. People came from all over the world to be a part of the nightly services, and it is estimated that around 200,000 gave their lives to the Lord. Miracles of the heart were among the most incredible to take place: hurt was healed, marriages were restored, and many were freed from the power of addiction. Some who came were healed physically just by walking into the room, struck by the presence of God. The harvest was plentiful, and finding workers was key to sustaining what God was doing. Teams were set up to focus on deliverance, intercession during the meetings, and ministry times at the front. A school was started, and many would be impacted by what God was doing, receiving calls to step into full-time ministry themselves. After five years a church split led to the eventual fading out of the movement. But there was no doubt about it: what was prophesied all those years ago came to pass because one church was hungry enough to see God's kingdom come and His will be done on earth as it is in heaven.[20] Are you?

HANDS-ON *Activity*

Look at a globe and choose a country to join with. Draw or design a flag that combines the two into one and come up with a name.

VOCABULARY

EARLY READER
suspicious: *not trusting of others*
successor: *the next person in line*

EARLY ELEMENTARY
successor: *the next person in line*
shrewd: *having the ability to make good decisions*

UPPER ELEMENTARY
shrewd: *having the ability to make good decisions*
conspiring: *secretly planning with other people to do something bad*

MIDDLE SCHOOL
conspiring: *secretly planning with other people to do something bad*
perilous: *very dangerous*

HIGH SCHOOL
perilous: *very dangerous*
assail: *violently attack*

Renaissance and Revival

LESSON 20: TURNING THE PAGE

It's hard to imagine that we are at the end of our unit. We have covered a lot of amazing people, and there are many more that we didn't have room for. As the Renaissance came to a close, the Scientific Revolution would burst forth into the Enlightenment. Some of the greatest minds of all time would carry the baton forward, such as Sir Isaac Newton, who would build on Galileo's discoveries. As we talked about in the first lesson, the lines are a bit blurry when it comes to the different periods. For example most historians agree that the Renaissance came to an end by the early 17th century, even though the Scientific Revolution overlapped with this time frame. In our final lesson we'll talk about one man who found himself right in the transition between these two periods. In fact, he is often considered one of the founders of the Scientific Revolution . . . meet Sir Francis Bacon.

A PHILOSOPHER, LAWYER, POLITICIAN, AND AUTHOR

Born on January 22, 1561, in London, England, Francis Bacon was a loyal member of the Church of England (which made him an Anglican). He had a relatively normal childhood, eventually going to school to study philosophy and law before becoming a lawyer at the age of 21. His critical thinking made him an **asset** not only to the field of law but to politics as well, and he eventually become a member of Parliament. Things were going well for Francis, and his future was looking promising until he got on the bad side of the queen by taking a position that was opposite of hers on a matter—not a smart move. To get himself back in her good graces, he befriended one of the queen's "favorites" (people she kept close to her) named the Earl of Essex, who recommended him for various positions in the court. In the end Francis' attempts were unsuccessful, as the queen apparently had a long memory, and his career came to a standstill. When King James came to power, however, everything started to change.

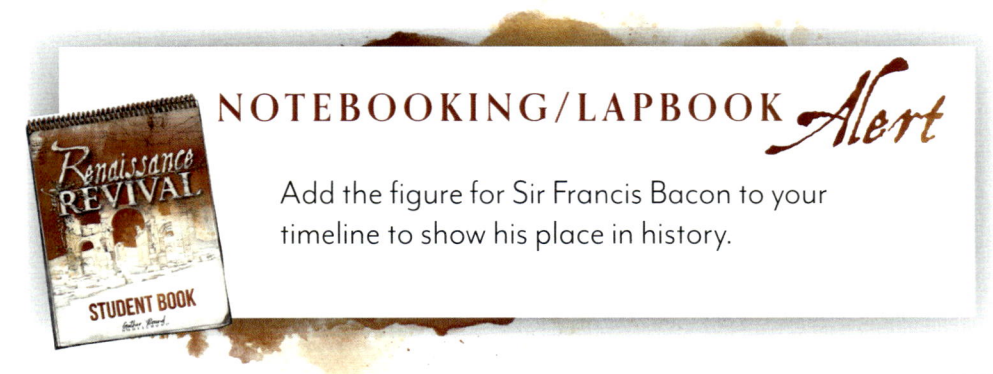

NOTEBOOKING/LAPBOOK *Alert*

Add the figure for Sir Francis Bacon to your timeline to show his place in history.

Like writing a cover letter for a résumé in order to describe your qualifications, Francis promoted himself through sending correspondence to the new king. He shared his ideas, opinions, and **counsel**, hoping to prove how useful he could be. This strategy, along with some recommendations from people in high places, seemed to work, and Francis found favor at last. He was knighted in 1603 and eventually promoted to the position of attorney general to the king (which was kind of like being the monarch's own personal lawyer). During this time, at the peak of his career, Francis wrote many different essays, **tracts**, and opinion pieces about politics and philosophy—some of which survive to this day. However, as we have learned, being at the top is dangerous, and Francis made some enemies, leading to his eventual **downfall**. When he was charged with taking bribes, he admitted that it was true, but he vehemently defended his case, trying to prove that it had not affected his judgment. The king refused to see him, and in the end, he was imprisoned for a time, struck from politics as well as the king's court, and fined with a very costly fee. Francis' political career was over.

> **DID YOU KNOW?** There is some speculation that Sir Francis Bacon was actually the son of Queen Elizabeth I. This theory is based on letters written between the two of them that leave room for mystery and **intrigue**. Considering that she publicly declared she would never marry because England was her husband and that she was called the Virgin Queen, many disagree, saying that the evidence is **circumstantial** at best. If Francis was her son, Elizabeth chose to never publicly declare him as such, even when she was on her deathbed and was forced to name her cousin in Scotland as her successor. What do you think? Is it true?

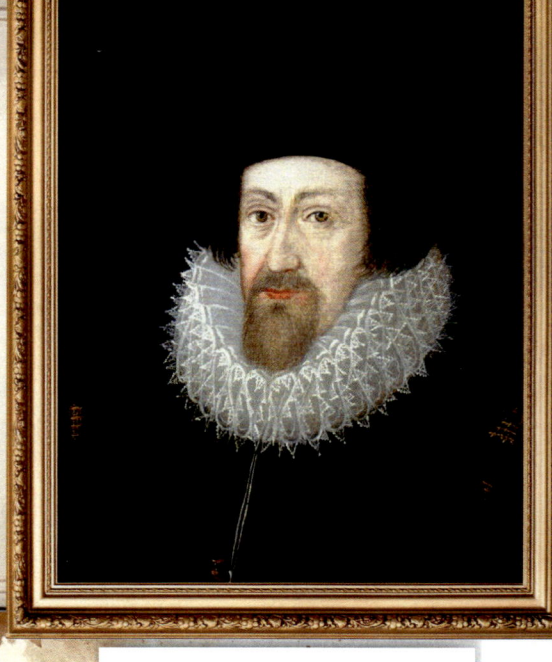

SIR FRANCIS BACON

OTHER CONTRIBUTIONS

After the untimely death of his political career, Francis found himself in a bit of a pickle. He had lost many valuable contacts, and his good name had been smeared. Nevertheless he persevered and continued to write. It was during this time that he created a history of Great Britain as well as books about the lives of some of the monarchs—just like Vasari had done! He pushed back against the education system and proposed that there needed to be change, arguing that dry philosophical debates and opinions were not effective and that educators should teach facts instead. His own distaste for some of what he went through in school contributed to his belief that experience was a far better teacher than lectures were. This idea led him to build on Galileo's more systematic approach to science by inventing the scientific method that we know and use today, which is sometimes called the Baconian method in his honor. Francis thought that everything should be doubted and proven with a hypothesis, variables, and tests. He believed that for the method to truly work and for the truth to be known, everyone needed to adopt these same standards for testing theories—an idea that wasn't fully accepted until much later. The fact that others weren't exactly on board didn't seem to deter him, and Francis used this new model with many different experiments. He was particularly interested in the impact that cold temperatures had on people, sickness, and decay—basically the idea of refrigeration. In one of his experiments where he stuffed a chicken with snow, Francis caught a chill. As he had always been prone to illness throughout his life, his cold turned into an infection, and he died a week later . . . leaving behind some of the most extraordinary works of philosophy, literature, and science of the Late Renaissance.

WHAT NEXT?

We have done an in-depth study of many different revivals, but we've barely scratched the surface. There are hundreds of accounts of God pouring out His Spirit on His people and meeting them in their hunger and humility—far more than we could fit into this unit. It is important to remember that God isn't finished with us yet! Each revival hit *suddenly*. They had been longed for, prayed for, and sought after . . . but they could not be fabricated or forced. Throughout history God has poured His Spirit out not because of people's merit but as a direct result of their humility and their hunger. The real question is, how bad do you want it? What will the next big revival story be? Maybe it will start with extraordinary prayer from just a few young people, or perhaps it will come from families gathering in His name—consecrated for Him. But when it does happen, remember that not everyone will receive it. There will always be those who are critical of movements, and people's own pride and sin often gets in the way, causing many churches to split and revivals to stop dead in their tracks. What's next is up to you. God is looking for a wholehearted, sold-out people who will pursue purity over publicity and choose faithfulness over fame. A renaissance of the human heart . . . the kind of revival that will bear fruit forever.

The men and women we have met in this unit had visions that were costly, requiring for some their very lives. And yet even the darkest of tragedies and the most foolish mistakes could be redeemed by a God who works all things together for good. Through these people's examples, we have the ability to look back and study, learn, and grow—to write a better story. What will you build on the foundations that have been laid? What will you stand for? What redemption will God work through and in your life? What dominos will be triggered because of *your* obedience? May you be a carrier of revival everywhere you go, bringing the new thing that God is doing into situations and speaking His life and power and hope to broken places. May *you* be the generation that changes the world.

VOCABULARY

EARLY READER
asset: *something that is useful*
counsel: *advice*

EARLY ELEMENTARY
counsel: *advice*
tract: *a small brochure that contains information about religion or politics*

UPPER ELEMENTARY
tract: *a small brochure that contains information about religion or politics*
circumstantial: *not completely accurate; based on coincidence*

MIDDLE SCHOOL
circumstantial: *not completely accurate; based on coincidence*
intrigue: *a fascinating quality*

HIGH SCHOOL
intrigue: *a fascinating quality*
downfall: *loss of power or status*

HANDS-ON Activity

Do you think experience is a better teacher than listening to someone teach *at* you? Try it! Choose something that you want to know more about and see if you can find a hands-on way to learn it. You could try filling up a tire with air, greasing your bike chain, cooking a new recipe, or going on a nature walk and sketching what you observe. What did you learn during your experience? Do you think you might remember it more than if someone had just told you about it? Why, or why not?

Appendix

Europe
REFERENCE MAP

LESSON 3 SERMON OF JOHN LIVINGSTONE—KIRK OF SHOTTS REVIVAL

"Ezekiel 36:25–26 (KJV): Then will I sprinkle clean water upon you, and ye shall be clean: from all your filthiness, and from all your idols, will I cleanse you. A new heart also will I give you, and a new spirit will I put within you: and I will take away the stony heart out of your flesh, and I will give you an heart of flesh.

If a few drops of rain so discompose you, how discomposed would you be, how full of horror and despair, if God should deal with you as you deserve? And God will deal thus with all the finally impenitent. God might justly rain fire and brimstone upon you, as he did upon Sodom and Gomorrah, and the other cities of the plain. But, for ever blessed be his name! the door of mercy still stands open for such as you are. The Son of God, by tabernacling in our nature, and obeying and suffering in it, is the only refuge and covert from the storm of divine wrath due to us for sin. His merits and mediation alone are the screen from that storm, and none but those who come to Christ just as they are, empty of everything, and take the offered mercy at his hand, will have the benefit of this shelter."[21]

LESSON 4

IN 1492
BY JEAN MARZOLLO

In fourteen hundred ninety-two
Columbus sailed the ocean blue.

He had three ships and left from Spain;
He sailed through sunshine, wind and rain.

He sailed by night; he sailed by day;
He used the stars to find his way.

A compass also helped him know
How to find the way to go.

Ninety sailors were on board;
Some men worked while others snored.

Then the workers went to sleep;
And others watched the ocean deep.

Day after day they looked for land;
They dreamed of trees and rocks and sand.

October 12 their dream came true,
You never saw a happier crew!

"Indians! Indians!" Columbus cried;
His heart was filled with joyful pride.

But "India" the land was not;
It was the Bahamas, and it was hot.

The Arakawa natives were very nice;
They gave the sailors food and spice.

Columbus sailed on to find some gold
To bring back home, as he'd been told.

He made the trip again and again,
Trading gold to bring to Spain.

The first American? No, not quite.
But Columbus was brave, and he was bright.[22]

Renaissance TIMELINE
1350–1650

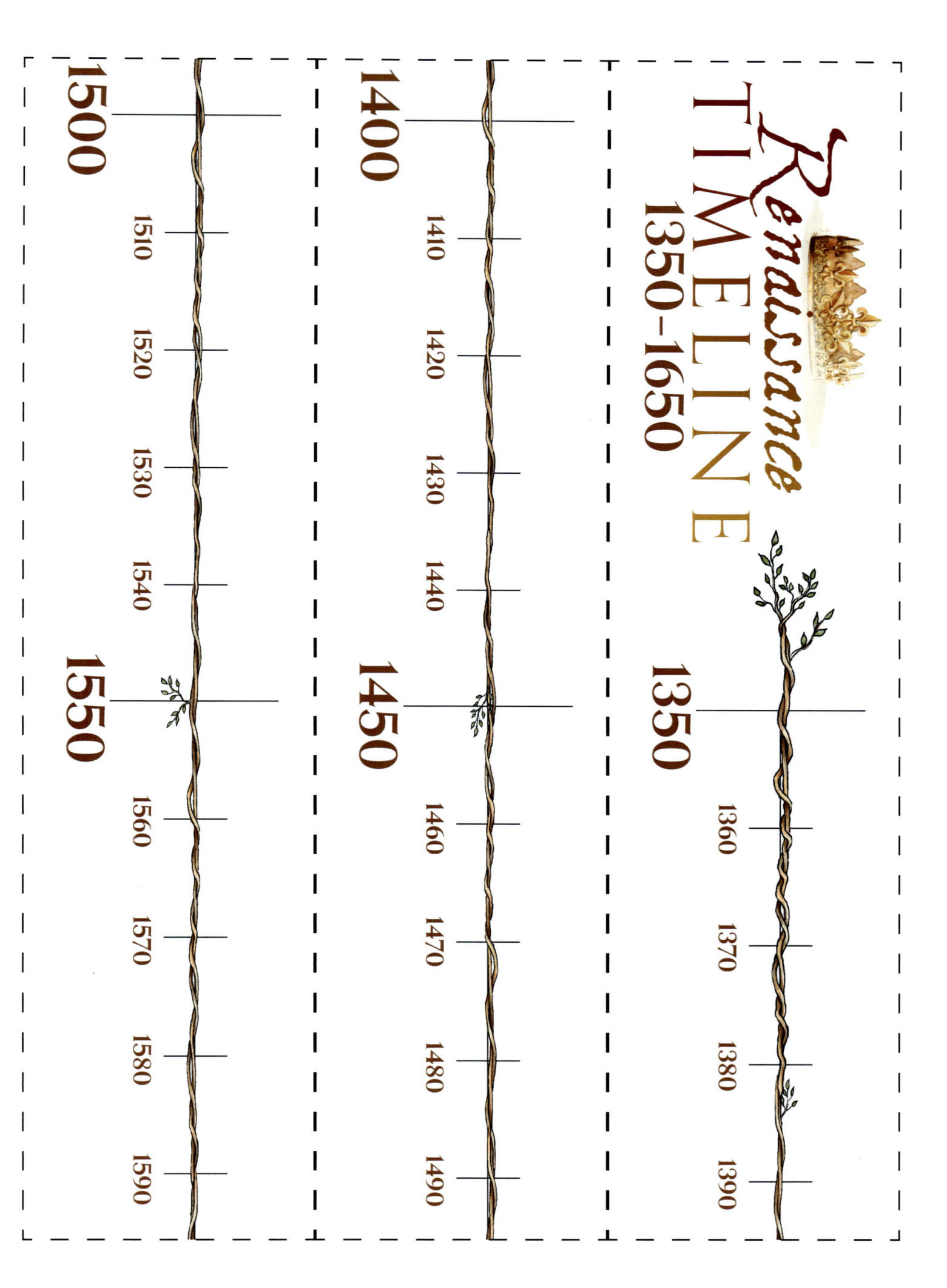

1350 — 1360 — 1370 — 1380 — 1390

1400 — 1410 — 1420 — 1430 — 1440 — **1450** — 1460 — 1470 — 1480 — 1490

1500 — 1510 — 1520 — 1530 — 1540 — **1550** — 1560 — 1570 — 1580 — 1590

1600 | 1610 | 1620 | 1630 | 1640 | 1650

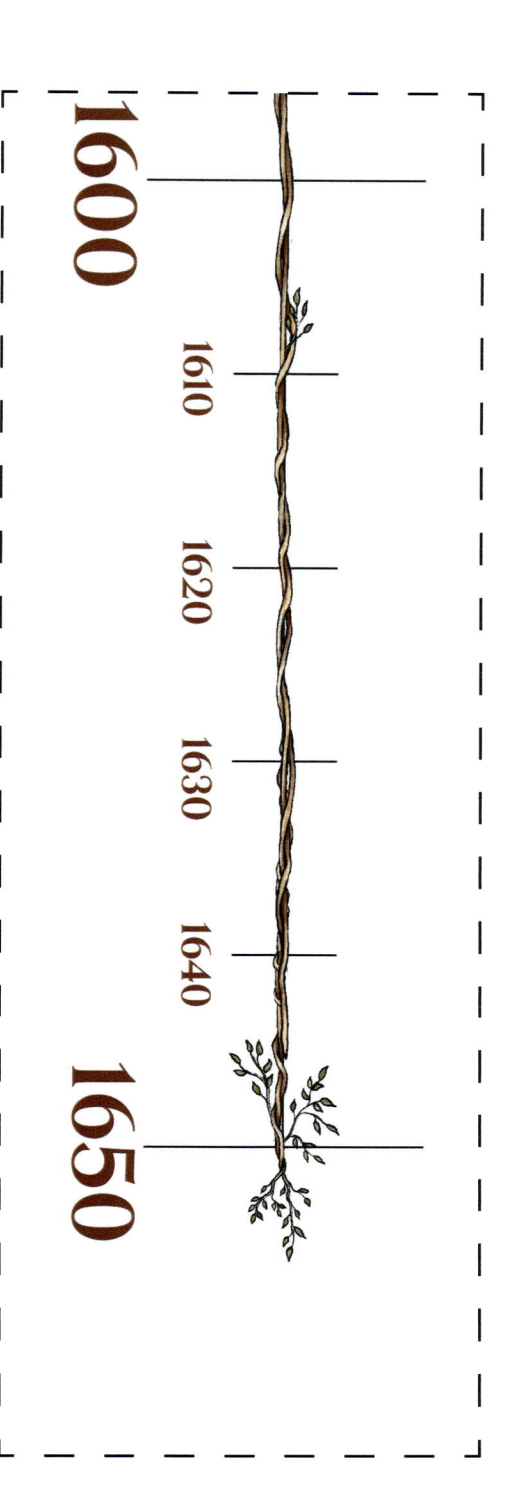

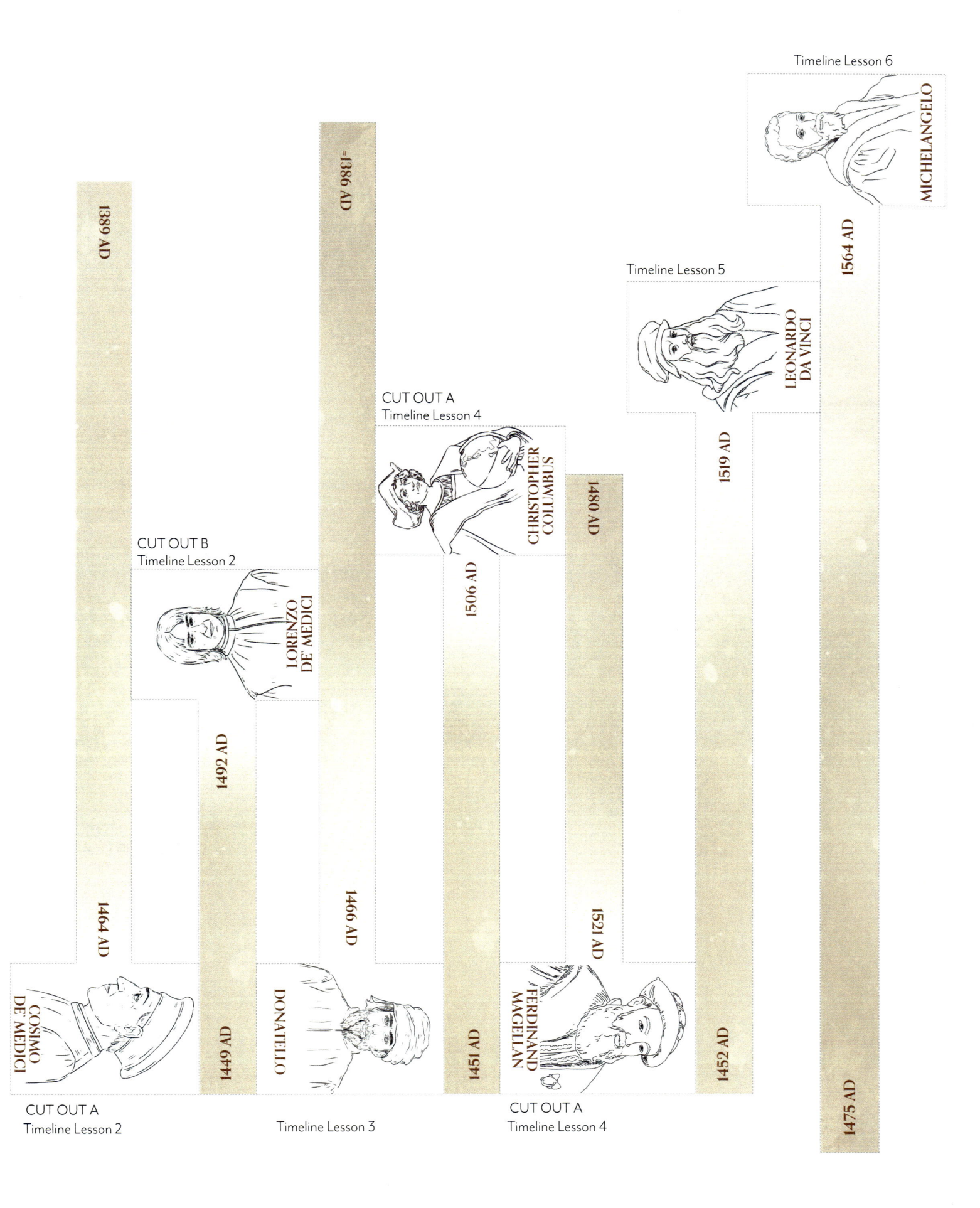

TIMELINE CUTOUTS

Timeline Lesson 6

MICHELANGELO
1564 AD

Timeline Lesson 5

LEONARDO DA VINCI
1519 AD

1386 AD

CUT OUT A
Timeline Lesson 4

CHRISTOPHER COLUMBUS
1506 AD

1480 AD

1389 AD

CUT OUT B
Timeline Lesson 2

LORENZO DE MEDICI
1492 AD

1466 AD

DONATELLO
1449 AD

FERDINAND MAGELLAN
1521 AD

1452 AD

1464 AD

COSIMO DE MEDICI

1451 AD

1475 AD

CUT OUT A
Timeline Lesson 2

Timeline Lesson 3

CUT OUT A
Timeline Lesson 4

TIMELINE CUTOUTS

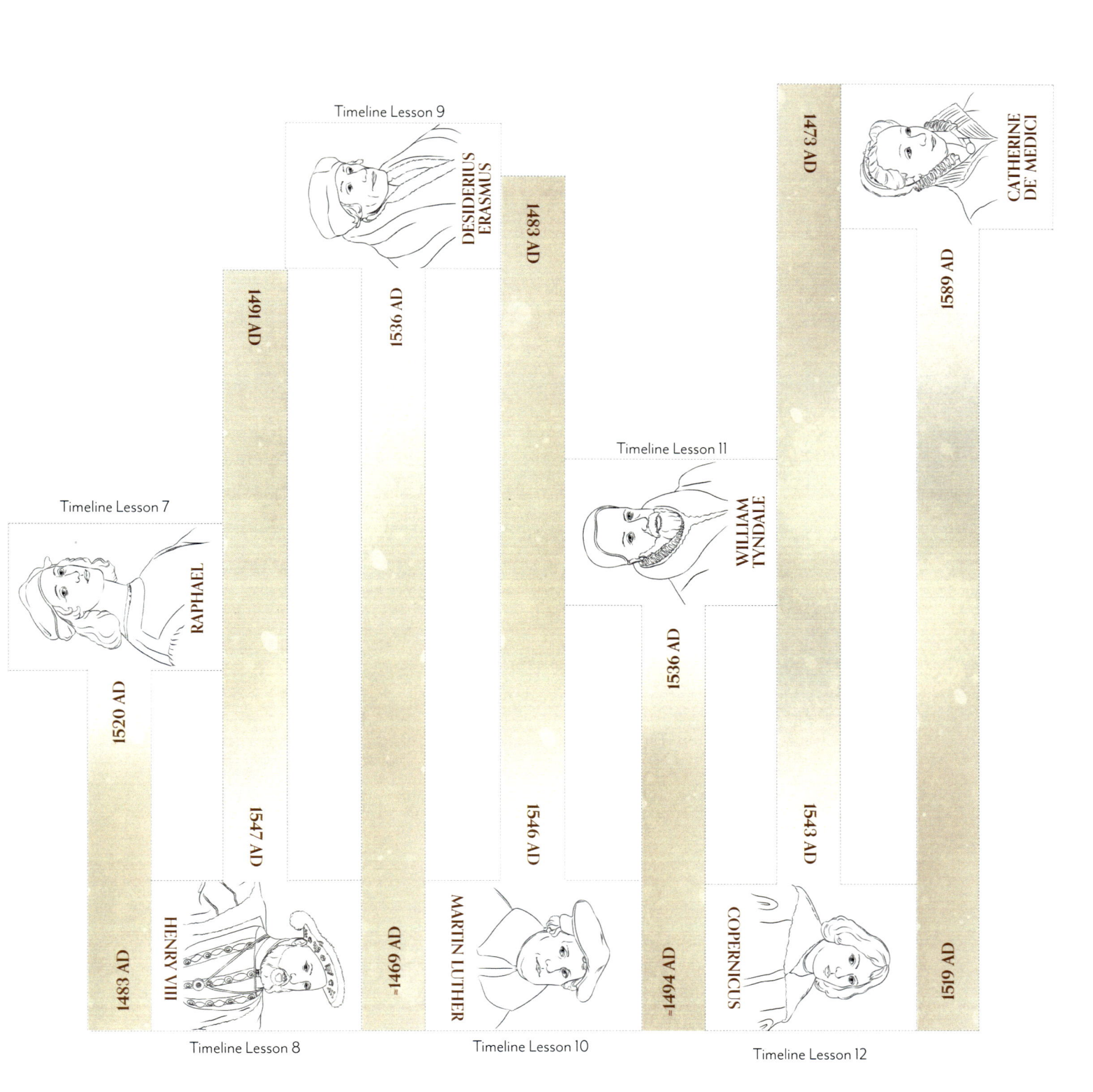

Timeline Lesson 7 — RAPHAEL — 1483 AD — 1520 AD

Timeline Lesson 8 — HENRY VIII — 1491 AD — 1547 AD

Timeline Lesson 9 — DESIDERIUS ERASMUS — 1469 AD — 1536 AD

Timeline Lesson 10 — MARTIN LUTHER — 1483 AD — 1546 AD

Timeline Lesson 11 — WILLIAM TYNDALE — 1494 AD — 1536 AD

Timeline Lesson 12 — COPERNICUS — 1473 AD — 1543 AD

CATHERINE DE' MEDICI — 1519 AD — 1589 AD

TIMELINE CUTOUTS

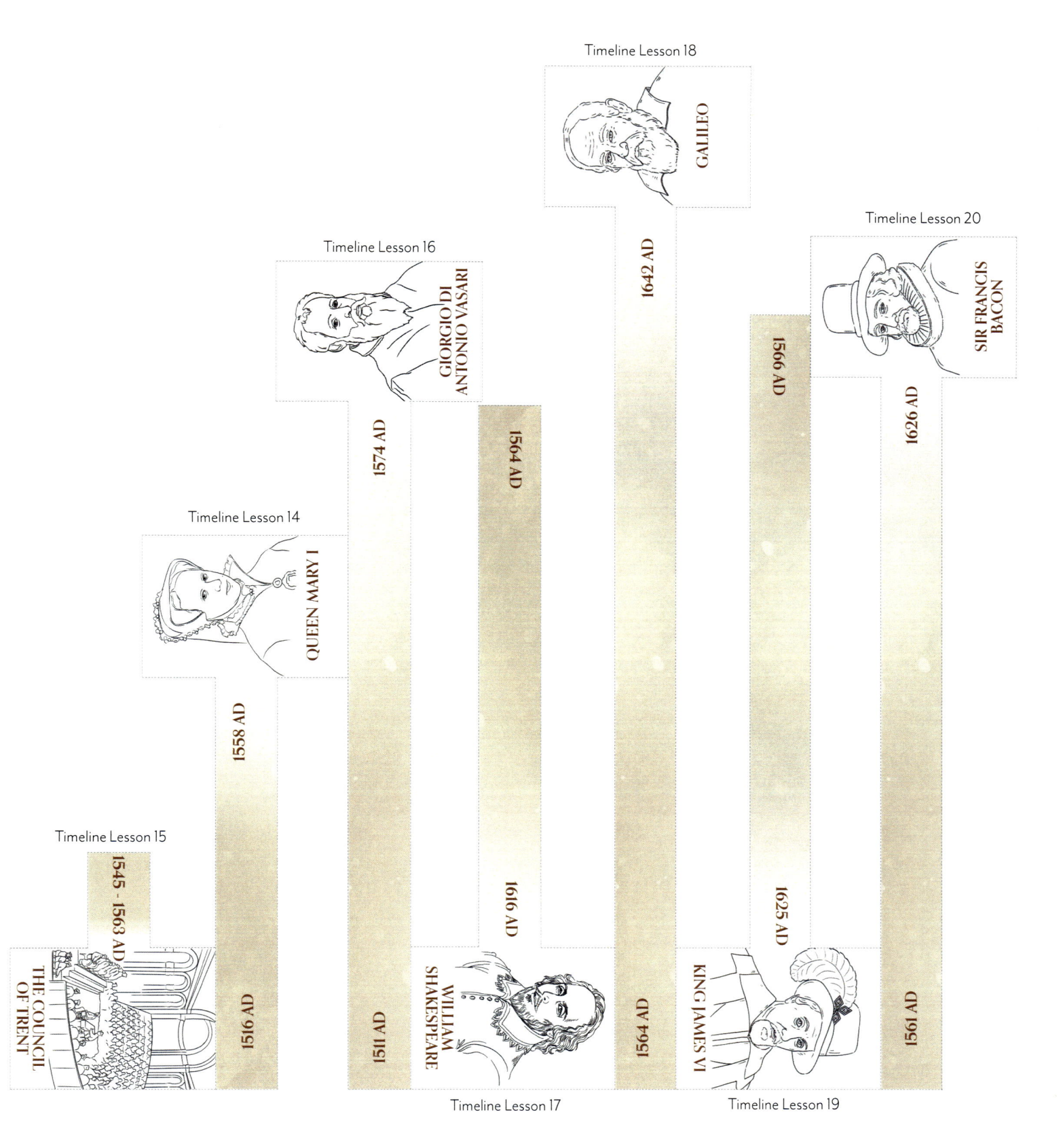

Timeline Lesson 14 — QUEEN MARY I — 1558 AD

Timeline Lesson 15 — THE COUNCIL OF TRENT — 1545 - 1563 AD — 1516 AD

Timeline Lesson 16 — GIORGIO DI ANTONIO VASARI — 1574 AD — 1564 AD

Timeline Lesson 17 — WILLIAM SHAKESPEARE — 1616 AD — 1511 AD

Timeline Lesson 18 — GALILEO — 1642 AD — 1564 AD

Timeline Lesson 19 — KING JAMES VI — 1625 AD — 1561 AD

Timeline Lesson 20 — SIR FRANCIS BACON — 1626 AD — 1566 AD

ENDNOTES

1. Exodus 33:11
2. Luke 12:7
3. Jeremiah 29:11
4. Bernard Shaw, *Man And Superman A Comedy And A Philosophy*, New York: Brentano's, 1905.
5. "Quotes of Michelangelo," Michelangelo.org, www.Michelangelo.org, Accessed October 8, 2023, https://www.michelangelo.org/michelangelo-quotes.jsp.
6. 2 Peter 3:9
7. 2 Peter 3:9
8. "Luther and the Thunderstorm," Ligonier Updates, Ligonier Ministries, October 25, 2019, https://www.ligonier.org/posts/luther-and-thunderstorm.
9. "The 95 Theses," www.LUTHER.de, KDG Wittenberg, Accessed October 25, 2023, https://www.luther.de/en/95thesen.html.
10. Peter J. Gurry, "The Life and Legacy of William Tyndale," Text & Canon Institute, Text & Canon Institute, May 3, 2022, https://textandcanon.org/the-life-and-legacy-of-william-tyndale/.
11. "The Life and Legacy of William Tyndale."
12. "Korean Revivals," ByFaith, ByFaith Media, Accessed October 29, 2023, https://www.byfaith.co.uk/paul20102.htm.
13. 2 Samuel 6:22a
14. "1953 Congo Revival," Beautiful Feet, Beautiful Feet, Accessed November 8, 2023, https://romans1015.com/1953-congo/.
15. "Michelangelo, Vasari & the Hall of a Hundred Days," Walks in Rome, David Lown, February 18, 2021, https://www.walksinrome.com/blog/frescoes-by-vasari-sala-dei-cento-giorni-palazzo-della-cancelleria-rome.
16. "1953 Congo Revival," Beautiful Feet, Beautiful Feet, Accessed November 8, 2023, https://romans1015.com/1953-congo/.
17. Exodus 3
18. Matthew 14:22-33
19. "1995 Cali, Columbia Revival," Beautiful Feet, Beautiful Feet, Accessed November 15, 2023, https://romans1015.com/cali/.
20. Matthew 6:10
21. ET staff writer. "Revival snapshots." Evangelical Times. Evangelical Times, June 1, 1997. https://www.evangelical-times.org/revival-snapshots/.
22. Marzollo, Jean. "In 1492." Your Daily Poem. Your Daily Poem, Accessed November 2, 2023. https://www.yourdailypoem.com/listpoem.jsp?poem_id=3144.

RESOURCES

Parent note: *Please note that many of these sources include original Renaissance artwork that contain nudity. If you are using these for research for your child, we recommend using the vetted links listed on the resource page on the app or you as a parent checking the links before referring them to your students.*

Lesson 1
Hunt, Dr. John M. "Humanism in renaissance Italy." Smarthistory. Smarthistory, August 1, 2021. https://smarthistory.org/humanism-renaissance-italy/.
Cartwright, Mark. "Renaissance Humanism." World History Encyclopedia. World History Encyclopedia, November 4, 2020. https://www.worldhistory.org/Renaissance_Humanism/.
The Editors of Encyclopædia Britannica. "Leaning Tower of Pisa." Britannica. The Encyclopædia Britannica, Inc., August 9, 2023. https://www.britannica.com/topic/Leaning-Tower-of-Pisa.

Lesson 2
"Medici Family." The Medici Family. The Medici Family, Accessed September 28, 2023. https://themedicifamily.com/.
The Editors of Encyclopædia Britannica. "Cosimo de' Medici." Britannica. Encyclopædia Britannica, Inc., September 23, 2023. https://www.britannica.com/biography/Cosimo-de-Medici.
"Lorenzo the Magnificent." Florence Inferno. Florence Inferno, March 15, 2017. https://www.florenceinferno.com/lorenzo-the-magnificent/.
"Why Was Lorenzo So Magnificent." Walks Inside Florence. Walks Inside Florence, Accessed September 28, 2023. https://www.walksinsideflorence.it/why-was-lorenzo-so-magnificent.html.
Wilkinson, Freddie. "The Protestant Reformation." National Geographic. National Geographic Society, June 2, 2022. https://education.nationalgeographic.org/resource/protestant-reformation/.
Mantegna, Andrea. "The Adoration of the Shepherds." The Met. The Metropolitan Museum of Art, Accessed September 28, 2023. https://www.metmuseum.org/art/collection/search/436966.

Lesson 3
Cartwright, Mark. "Donatello." World History Encyclopedia. World History Encyclopedia, August 26, 2020. https://www.worldhistory.org/Donatello/.
Draper, James David. "Donatello (ca. 1386–1466)" The MET. The Metropolitan Museum of Art, October 2002. https://www.metmuseum.org/toah/hd/dona/hd_dona.htm.
"Donatello Biography." Donatello.net. Present www.Donatello.net, Accessed October 1, 2023. https://www.donatello.net/.
"Donatello." The Art Story. The Art Story Foundation, Accessed October 1, 2023. https://www.theartstory.org/artist/donatello/.
History.com Editors. "Printing Press." History. A&E Television Networks, LLC., June 29, 2023. https://www.history.com/topics/inventions/printing-press.
ET staff writer. "Revival snapshots." Evangelical Times. Evangelical Times, June 1, 1997. https://www.evangelical-times.org/revival-snapshots/.

Lesson 4
"Christopher Columbus." Royal Museums Greenwich. Royal Museums Greenwich, Accessed October 3, 2023. https://www.rmg.co.uk/stories/topics/christopher-columbus.
"Ferdinand Magellan (1480 - 1521)" BBC. BBC, Accessed October 3, 2023. https://www.bbc.co.uk/history/historic_figures/magellan_ferdinand.shtml.
"What is a mariner's astrolabe?" Royal Museums Greenwich. Royal Museums Greenwich, Accessed October 3, 2023. https://www.rmg.co.uk/stories/topics/what-mariners-astrolabe.
"Martin Behaim's 'Erdapfel', the Oldest Surviving Terrestrial Globe." HistoryofInformation.com. Jeremy M. Norman, Accessed October 3, 2023. https://www.historyofinformation.com/detail.php?id=3611.
"Moravian Revival of 1727 (expanded version)." Beautiful Feet. Beautiful Feet, Accessed October 3, 2023. https://romans1015.com/moravian-revival-2/.

Lesson 5
Robinson, Megan D. "The Mona Lisa: A Brief History of da Vinci's Famous Painting." Art & Object. Journalistic, Inc., May 5, 2023. https://www.artandobject.com/news/mona-lisa-brief-history-da-vincis-famous-painting.
"Activity: Mirror Writing." Museum of Science. Museum of Science, Boston, Accessed October 6, 2023. https://www.mos.org/leonardo/activities/mirror-riting.
"1708 Silesian Children's Prayer Revival." Beautiful Feet. Beautiful Feet, Accessed October 6, 2023. https://romans1015.com/silesian/.
Mussio, Gina. "The Life of Leonardo Da Vinci: 9 Facts They Didn't Teach You in School." Walks of Italy. Walks of Italy, June 19, 2023. https://www.walksofitaly.com/blog/art-culture/leonardo-da-vinci-surprising-facts.

Lesson 5, cont.
Nardini, Bruno. "Leonardo da Vinci as told to children." UNESCO. UNESCO, Accessed October 8, 2023. https://en.unesco.org/courier/october-1974/leonardo-da-vinci-told-children.

Lesson 6
Nicole, April. "The Life & Art of Michelangelo Buonarroti." What a Life Tours. What a Life Tours LLC, May 28, 2019. https://www.whatalifetours.com/blog-life-of-michelangelo-buonarroti/.
Andrews, Evan. "9 Things You May Not Know About Michelangelo." History. A&E Television Networks, LLC., August 7, 2023. https://www.history.com/news/9-things-you-may-not-know-about-michelangelo.
Landes, Nora. "The Forgery That Earned Michelangelo His First Roman Patron." Artsy. Artsy, August 10, 2016. https://www.artsy.net/article/artsy-editorial-how-michelangelo-got-his-start-by-forging-antiquities.
"Michelangelo." Sistine Chapel. Sistine Chapel Rome, Accessed October 8, 2023. https://www.thesistinechapel.org/michelangelo.
History.com Editors. "Michelangelo is born." History. A&E Television Networks, LLC., March 4, 2021. https://www.history.com/this-day-in-history/michelangelo-born.
"The Life of Michelangelo." The Museums of Florence. Hidden Italy, Accessed October 8, 2023. http://www.museumsinflorence.com/foto/Accademia/Small/michelangelo.html.
"Quotes of Michelangelo." Michelangelo.org. www.Michelangelo.org, Accessed October 8, 2023. https://www.michelangelo.org/michelangelo-quotes.jsp.
Shirbon, Estelle. "Michelangelo more a prince than a pauper." Los Angeles Times. Los Angeles Times, December 3, 2002. https://www.latimes.com/archives/la-xpm-2002-dec-03-et-shirbon3-story.html.
"1820–1830s Revival on the Scottish Island of Lewis." Beautiful Feet. Beautiful Feet, Accessed October 8, 2023. https://romans1015.com/lewis-revival-1820s/.

Lesson 7
"Raphel." The Art Story. The Art Story Foundation, Accessed October 11, 2023. https://www.theartstory.org/artist/raphael/.
"Raphael Sanzio (1483-1520)." Old Master Print. Oldmasterprint, Accessed October 11, 2023. https://www.oldmasterprint.net/artist/raphael-sanzio-1483-1520.html.
"Raffello Sanzio, The Transfiguration." Musei Vaticani. Musei Vaticani, Accessed October 11, 2023. https://m.museivaticani.va/content/museivaticani-mobile/en/collezioni/musei/la-pinacoteca/sala-viii---secolo-xvi/raffaello-sanzio--trasfigurazione.html.
"Transfiguration." Totally History. Totallyhistory.com, Accessed October 11, 2023. https://totallyhistory.com/transfiguration/.
"1790-1840: Second Great Awakening." Beautiful Feet. Beautiful Feet, Accessed October 11, 2023. https://romans1015.com/2nd-awakening/.
"1815-1840 Upstate New York Revivals." Beautiful Feet. Beautiful Feet, Accessed October 11, 2023. https://romans1015.com/upstate-ny-revivals-2/.
"1801 Cane Ridge Revival." Beautiful Feet. Beautiful Feet, Accessed October 11, 2023. https://romans1015.com/cane-ridge/.

Lesson 8
"Henry VIII: Renaissance Prince or Terrible Tudor? Who Was the Real Henry VIII?" Historic Royal Palaces. Historic Royal Palaces, Accessed October 16, 2023. https://www.hrp.org.uk/hampton-court-palace/history-and-stories/henry-viii/.
"The Six Wives of Henry VIII." Thirteen PBS. Educational Broadcasting Corporation, Accessed October 16, 2023. https://www.thirteen.org/wnet/sixwives/meet/ca_handbook_why.html.
Soaft, Lucy. "The 5 Monarchs of the Tudor Period: An Overview." The Collector. TheCollector, December 18, 2022. https://www.thecollector.com/five-tudor-monarchs-tudor-period/.
Ridgway, Claire. "The Pregnancies of Katherine of Aragon by Sarah Bryson." The Tudor Society. The Tudor Society, Accessed October 16, 2023. https://www.tudorsociety.com/

RESOURCES

the-pregnancies-of-katherine-of-aragon-by-sarah-bryson/.
Brain, Jessica. "Sir Thomas More." Historic UK. Historic UK Ltd., Accessed October 16, 2023. https://www.historic-uk.com/HistoryUK/HistoryofBritain/Sir-Thomas-More/.
History.com Editors. "Church of England." History. A&E Television Networks LLC., February 13, 2018. https://www.history.com/topics/european-history/church-of-england.
"1836 Hawaiian Revival." Beautiful Feet. Beautiful Feet, Accessed October 16, 2023. https://romans1015.com/1836-hawaiian-revival/.

Lesson 9
"Desiderius Erasmus (1468?–1536)" Internet Encyclopedia of Philosophy. Internet Encyclopedia of Philosophy, Accessed October 23, 2023. https://iep.utm.edu/erasmus/.
Cartwright, Mark. ""Desiderius Erasmus." World History Encyclopedia. World History Encyclopedia, October 28, 2020. https://www.worldhistory.org/Desiderius_Erasmus/.
Cheah, Fook Meng. "A Review of Luther and Erasmus: Free Will and Salvation." PRCA. Protestant Reformed Churches in America, Accessed October 23, 2023. https://www.prca.org/prtj/nov95b.html.
"Titan and his paintings." Titan.org. www.Titan.org, Accessed October 23, 2023. https://www.titian.org/.
"1862 The Great Revival in the Confederate Armies." The Beautiful Feet. The Beautiful Feet, Accessed October 23, 2023. https://romans1015.com/1863-civil-war-revival/.
Woodworth, Steven E. "Religious Revivals during the Civil War." Encyclopedia Virginia. VIrginia Humanities, Accessed October 23, 2023. https://encyclopediavirginia.org/entries/religious-revivals-during-the-civil-war/.

Lesson 10
"Luther and the Thunderstorm." Ligonier Updates. Ligonier Ministries, October 15, 2019. https://www.ligonier.org/posts/luther-and-thunderstorm.
"Martin Luther (1483–1546)." Internet Encyclopedia of Philosophy. Internet Encyclopedia of Philosophy, Accessed October 25, 2023. https://iep.utm.edu/luther/.
"The 95 Theses." www.LUTHER.de. KDG Wittenberg, Accessed October 25, 2023. https://www.luther.de/en/95thesen.html.
Serge, Joseph. "Martin Luther and the Holocaust." The Canadian Jewish News. The Canadian Jewish News, October 28, 2019. https://thecjn.ca/perspectives/martin-luther-and-the-holocaust/.
"The Welsh Revival of 1904-05." Beautiful Feet. Beautiful Feet, Accessed October 25, 2023. https://romans1015.com/welsh-revival-1904-05/.
Stead, William T., G. Campbell Morgan, Arthur Goodrich, and Evan Roberts. *The Welsh Revival & The Story of The Welsh Revival: As Told by Eyewitnesses Together With a Sketch of Evan Roberts and His Message to The World*. Lawton, OK: Trumpet Press, 2015.

Lesson 11
Gurry, Peter J. "The Life and Legacy of William Tyndale." Text & Canon Institute. Text & Canon Institute, May 3, 2022. https://textandcanon.org/the-life-and-legacy-of-william-tyndale/.
Piper, John. "William Tyndale: A Life Transformed by God's Word." Desiring God. Desiring God, May 26, 2008. https://www.desiringgod.org/messages/william-tyndale-a-life-transformed-by-gods-word.
"1903 Wonsan, Korea Revival." Beautiful Feet. Beautiful Feet, Accessed October 29, 2023. https://romans1015.com/1903-wonsan-korea/.
"1907-1910 Pyongyang Korea Revival. Beautiful Feet. Beautiful Feet, Accessed October 29, 2023. https://romans1015.com/1907-pyongyang-revival/.
"Korean Revivals." By Faith. By Faith Ministries. Accessed October 29, 2023. https://www.byfaith.co.uk/paul20102.htm.

Lesson 12
Rabin, Sheila. "Nicolaus Copernicus." Stanford Encyclopedia of Philosophy. The Metaphysics Research Lab, Department of Philosophy, Stanford University, Accessed November 1, 2023. https://plato.stanford.edu/entries/copernicus/.
The Editors of Encyclop dia Britannica. "Sigismund I." Britannica. Encyclop dia Britannica, Inc., March 28, 2023. https://www.britannica.com/biography/Sigismund-I-king-of-Poland. "Renaissance in Poland." Academic Accelerator. Academic Accelerator, Accessed November 1, 2023. https://academic-accelerator.com/encyclopedia/renaissance-in-poland.
"Zamosc, Poland – A Pearl of the Renaissance." World Traveler. World Traveler, Accessed November 1, 2023. https://worldtraveler.travel/zamosc-poland-a-pearl-of-the-renaissance/.
"1905-1906 Khasi Hills Revival." Beautiful Feet. Beautiful Feet, Accessed November 1, 2023. https://romans1015.com/1905-khasi-hills-revival/.

Lesson 13
"A Girl in Renaissance Europe." Girl Museum. Girl Museum, May 23, 2014. https://www.girlmuseum.org/a-girl-in-renaissance-europe/.
"Catherine de' Medici." University of Michigan Museum of Art. The Regents of the University of Michigan, Accessed November 3, 2023. https://umma.umich.edu/archive/view/ONLINE/women/real_stories/profiles/catherine.htm.
Mark, Joshua J. "Catherine de' Medici." World History Encyclopedia. World History Encyclopedia, June 22, 2022. https://www.worldhistory.org/Catherine_de'_Medici/.
"The whole story of Catherine de Medici." Firenze. Gruppo Editoriale, April 8, 2019. https://www.firenzemadeintuscany.com/en/article/catherine-medici-history-florence/.
Marsh, Janine. "History of the Louvre Museum, Paris." The Good Life France. The Good Life France, Accessed November 3, 2023. https://thegoodlifefrance.com/history-of-the-louvre-museum-paris/.
"10 cool facts about the Louvre." LivTours. LivTours, February 21, 2022. https://livtours.com/blog/10-cool-facts-about-the-louvre/.
"1948 Latter Rain Revival." Beautiful Feet. Beautiful Feet, Accessed November 3, 2023. https://romans1015.com/latter-rain/.

Lesson 14
"Mary I (r.1553-1558)." Royal.uk. The Royal Household, Accessed November 6, 2023. https://www.royal.uk/mary-i.
"Elizabeth I: Was Elizabeth's 44-Year Reign Really a 'Golden Era' of English History?" Historic Royal Palaces. Historic Royal Palaces, Accessed November 6, 2023. https://www.hrp.org.uk/hampton-court-palace/history-and-stories/elizabeth-i/.
"Revival on the Island of Lewis: 1949-1952." Beautiful Feet. Beautiful Feet, Accessed November 6, 2023. https://romans1015.com/lewis-revival/.
Smithers, David. "The Intercessors of the Hebrides Revival." EvanWiggs.com. Measure of Gold Revival Ministries, Accessed November 6, 2023. http://www.evanwiggs.com/revival/history/hebpray.html.
"The amazing story of the Trump family Bible and its revival connection." Metro Voice. Metro Voice Newspaper, April 23, 2020. https://metrovoicenews.com/the-amazing-story-of-the-trump-family-bible-and-its-revival-connection/.
"A guide to coronations." Westminster Abbey. Dean and Chapter of Westminster, Accessed November 6, 2023. https://www.westminster-abbey.org/history/coronations-at-the-abbey/a-guide-to-coronations.
"What is a Coronation?" Royal Collection Trust. The Royal Collection Trust, Accessed November 6, 2023. https://www.rct.uk/discover/school-resources/what-is-a-coronation.
Rotondi, Jessica Pearce. "5 Objects used in British Royal Ceremonies and Their Symbolism." History. A&E Television Networks, LLC., May 4, 2023. https://www.history.com/news/british-royal-ceremony-funeral-coronation-objects.

Lesson 15
"Paul III." Student's Guide to Italian Renaissance Literature. Student's Guide to Italian Renaissance Literature, Accessed November 9, 2023. https://www.sgira.org/pope_paul_3.htm.
McDowell, Mark. "The Regensburg Colloquy (1541)." reformation21. Alliance of Confessing Evangelicals, Inc., February 12, 2016. https://www.reformation21.org/articles/the-regensburg-colloquy-1541.php.
The Editors of Encyclop dia Britannica. "Counter-Reformation." Britannica. Encyclop dia Britannica, Inc., October 9, 2023. https://www.britannica.com/event/Counter-Reformation.
Nichols, Steven, host. "The Council of Trent." 5 Minutes in Church History (podcast). January 20, 2016. https://www.ligonier.org/podcasts/5-minutes-in-church-history-with-stephen-nichols/the-council-of-trent.
Emmons, D.D. "Myths and Facts About the Council of Trent." Simply Catholic. Our Sunday Visitor, Accessed November 8, 2023. https://www.simplycatholic.com/myths-and-facts-about-the-council-of-trent/.
Mark, Joshua J. "Index of Prohibited Books." World History Encyclopedia. World History Encyclopedia, June 21, 2022. https://www.worldhistory.org/article/2018/index-of-prohibited-books/.
D'Emilio, Frances. "Vatican Looks Back At Inquisition." CBS News. CBS Interactive Inc., June 15, 2004. https://www.cbsnews.com/news/vatican-looks-back-at-inquisition/.
"Biblioteca Marciana." History of Library Architecture. Wordpress, Accessed November 8, 2023. https://historyoflibraryarchitecture.wordpress.com/16th-century/biblioteca-marciana/.
Goldman, Sydney. "Saint Mark's Library." A Global Renaissance. Wordpress, Accessed November 8, 2023. https://theglobalrenaissance.blog/home/saint-marks-library/.
"How Was Venice Built? Short History of Italy's Floating City." LivItaly Tours. LivItaly Tours, July 19, 2017. https://www.livitaly.com/how-was-venice-built/.
"The 1953 Congo Revival." Measure of Gold Revival Ministries. Measure of Gold Revival Ministries, Accessed November 8, 2023. http://www.evanwiggs.com/revival/history/1953%20

RESOURCES

Congo%20Revival.htm.
"1953 Congo Revival." Beautiful Feet. Beautiful Feet, Accessed November 8, 2023. https://romans1015.com/1953-congo/.
"History of Venice." Civitatis. Civitatis Tours, Accessed November 13, 20023. https://www.introducingvenice.com/history.

Lesson 16
"Giorgio Vasari." National Gallery of Art. National Gallery of Art, Accessed November 10, 2023. https://www.nga.gov/collection/artist-info.3269.html.
"Sala dei Cento Giorni - Palazzo della Cancelleria - Rome." akg-images. akg-images, Accessed November 10, 2023. https://www.akg-images.com/archive/Sala-dei-Cento-Giorni---Palazzo-della-Cancelleria---Rome-2UMEBM5UOUVLB.html.
Jakucewicz, Artur. "Giorgio Vasari." Italy4.Me. Italy for me, Accessed November 10, 2023. https://en.italy4.me/famous-italians/giorgio-vasari.html.
"Art in Tuscany." Traveling in Tuscany. The Academia, Accessed November 10, 2023. http://www.travelingintuscany.com/art/gutenberg/vasarilives.htm.
"1967-1972 The Jesus Movement." Beautiful Feet. Beautiful Feet, Accessed November 10, 2023. https://romans1015.com/jesus-movement/.

Lesson 17
"Shakespeare's Life and Times." Royal Shakespeare Company. Royal Shakespeare Company, Accessed November 14, 2023. https://www.rsc.org.uk/shakespeares-life-and-times.
"When Was Shakespeare Born?" Shakespeare Birthplace Trust. Shakespeare Birthplace Trust, Accessed November 14, 2023. https://www.shakespeare.org.uk/explore-shakespeare/shakespedia/william-shakespeare/when-was-shakespeare-born/.
"John Shakespeare." Shakespeare Birthplace Trust. Shakespeare Birthplace Trust, Accessed November 14, 2023. https://www.shakespeare.org.uk/explore-shakespeare/shakespedia/william-shakespeare/william-shakespeares-family/john-shakespeare/.
"The Globe." The Shakespeare Globe Trust. The Shakespeare Globe Trust, Accessed November 14, 2023. https://www.shakespearesglobe.com/discover/shakespeares-world/the-globe/.
The Editors of Encyclopædia Britannica. "Globe Theatre." Britannica. Encyclopædia Britannica, Inc., November 11, 2023. https://www.britannica.com/topic/Globe-Theatre.
"1965 Timor Revival." Beautiful Feet. Beautiful Feet, Accessed November 14, 2023. https://romans1015.com/1965-timor-revival/.
"1965 Revival on Timor (the Controversy)." Beautiful Feet. Beautiful Feet, Accessed November 14, 2023. https://romans1015.com/timor-revival-controversy/.

Lesson 18
"Galileo Galilei (1564-1642)." National Library of Medicine. National Library of Medicine, Accessed November 15, 2023. https://www.ncbi.nlm.nih.gov/pmc/articles/PMC2564400/.
History.com Editors. "Galileo Galilei." History. A&E Television Networks LLC., June 6, 2023. https://www.history.com/topics/inventions/galileo-galilei.
"Marina Gamba." Museo Galileo. IMSS, Accessed November 15, 2023. https://brunelleschi.imss.fi.it/itineraries/biography/marinagamba.html.
"Galileo Galilei." Stanford Encyclopedia of Philosophy. The Metaphysics Research Lab, Department of Philosophy, Stanford University, June 4, 2021. https://plato.stanford.edu/entries/galileo/.
"Galileo and the Telescope." Library of Congress. Library of Congress, Accessed November 15, 2023. https://www.loc.gov/collections/finding-our-place-in-the-cosmos-with-carl-sagan/articles-and-essays/modeling-the-cosmos/galileo-and-the-telescope.
"1995 Cali, Columbia Revival." Beautiful Feet. Beautiful Feet, Accessed November 15, 2023. https://romans1015.com/cali/.
Ruibal, Ruth. "Revival impacted Bolivia." Renewal Journal. Renewal Journal, January 13, 2014. https://renewaljournal.com/2014/01/13/revival-impacted-bolivia-byruth-ruibal/.
"DAY 32 – Bolivia's Apostle of the Andes." The Jesus Fast. The Jesus Fast, September 16, 2020. https://thejesusfast.global/day-32-bolivias-apostle-of-the-andes/.
"The Marks of Genuine Revival Shared by Julio Ruibal." True Light Miristries. True Light Ministries, July 24, 2022. https://www.truelightministries.org/post/the-marks-of-genuine-revival-shared-by-julio-ruibal.

Lesson 19
"King James VI/I." Undiscovered Scotland. Undiscovered Scotland, Accessed November 17, 2023. https://www.undiscoveredscotland.co.uk/usbiography/monarchs/jamesvi.html.
Matthew, David. "James I." Britannica. Encycopædia Britannica, Inc., October 15, 2023. https://www.britannica.com/biography/James-I-king-of-England-and-Scotland.
"James VI and Witchcraft." Philippa Gregory. Philippa Gregory, Accessed November 17, 2023. September 11, 2018. https://www.philippagregory.com/news/james-vi-and-witchcraft.
"James I and Anne of Denmark." Historic Royal Palaces. Historic Royal Palaces, Accessed November 17, 2023. https://www.hrp.org.uk/banqueting-house/history-and-stories/james-i-and-anne-of-denmark/.
Goodare, Julian. "A royal obsession with black magic started Europe's most brutal witch hunts." National Geographic. National Geographic Society, October 17, 2019. https://www.nationalgeographic.co.uk/history-and-civilisation/2019/10/royal-obsession-black-magic-started-europes-most-brutal-witch.
"What is the story behind Bonfire Night?" Royal Museums Greenwich. Royal Museums Greenwich, Accessed November 17, 2023. https://www.rmg.co.uk/stories/topics/gunpowder-plot-what-history-behind-bonfire-night.
Cavendish, Richard. "The First Union Flag." History Today. History Today Ltd., April 4, 2006. https://www.historytoday.com/archive/first-union-flag.
"1995 – Brownsville Revival." Beautiful Feet. Beautiful Feet, Accessed November 17, 2023. https://romans1015.com/brownsville-revival/.

Lesson 20
Quinton, Anthony M., Baron Quinton, Kathleen Marguerite Lea, and Peter Michael Urbach. "Francis Bacon." Britannica. Encyclopædia Britannica, Inc., October 11, 2023. https://www.britannica.com/biography/Francis-Bacon-Viscount-Saint-Alban.
Rodriguez, Kim. "2.1: What are the educational milestones of the 17th and 18th centuries?" LibreTexts Social Sciences. LibreTexts, Accessed November 19, 2023. https://socialsci.libretexts.org/Courses/Fresno_City_College/Education.
Wolford, Dr. Kathryn. "Francis Bacon and the scientific revolution." Khan Academy. Khan Academy, Accessed November 19, 2023. https://www.khanacademy.org/humanities/renaissance-reformation/baroque-art1/beginners-guide-baroque1/a/francis-bacon-and-the-scientific-revolution.
"Francis Bacon." Biography. Hearst Magazine Media, Inc., August 9, 2023. https://www.biography.com/scholars-educators/francis-bacon.

IMAGE RESOURCES

Lesson 2
Lorenzo de Medici: Workshop of Bronzino, Public domain, via Wikimedia Commons, https://upload.wikimedia.org/wikipedia/commons/1/10/Lorenzo_de_Medici.jpg.
The Adoration of the Shepherds: Andrea Mantegna, Public domain, via Wikimedia Commons, https://upload.wikimedia.org/wikipedia/commons/e/e0/1451_Mantegna_Die_Anbetung_der_Hirten_Metropolitan_Museum_of_Art_anagoria.jpg.

Lesson 3
Statue of David: Donatello, CC BY-SA 2.0 <https://creativecommons.org/licenses/by-sa/2.0>, via Wikimedia Commons, https://upload.wikimedia.org/wikipedia/commons/f/f0/Donatello_-_David_-_Floren%C3%A7a.jpg.

Lesson 5
Leonardo da Vinci: Leonardo da Vinci, Public domain, via Wikimedia Commons, https://upload.wikimedia.org/wikipedia/commons/b/ba/Leonardo_self.jpg.

Lesson 6
Michelangelo Daniele da Volterra: Daniele da Volterra, Public domain, via Wikimedia Commons, https://commons.wikimedia.org/wiki/File:Michelangelo_Daniele_da_Volterra_(dettaglio).jpg.

Lesson 7
Raffaello Sanzio: Raphael, Public domain, via Wikimedia Commons, https://upload.wikimedia.org/wikipedia/commons/f/f6/Raffaello_Sanzio.jpg.
The Transfiguration of Jesus: Raphael, Public domain, via Wikimedia Commons, https://upload.wikimedia.org/wikipedia/commons/5/51/Transfiguration_Raphael.jpg.
Camp Meeting: Bridport, Hugh, 1794-ca. 1868, lithographer, Public domain, via Wikimedia Commons, https://upload.wikimedia.org/wikipedia/commons/3/37/Camp_meeting.jpg.
Charles G. Finney: See page for author, Public domain, via Wikimedia Commons, https://upload.wikimedia.org/wikipedia/commons/9/96/Charles_g_finney.jpg.

Lesson 8
Portrait of Henry VIII: After Hans Holbein the Younger, Public domain, via Wikimedia Commons, https://upload.wikimedia.org/wikipedia/commons/f/f9/After_Hans_Holbein_the_Younger_-_Portrait_of_Henry_VIII_-_Google_Art_Project.jpg.

Lesson 9
Portrait of Desiderius Erasmus of Rotterdam with Renaissance Pilaster: Hans Holbein the Younger, Public domain, via Wikimedia Commons, https://upload.wikimedia.org/wikipedia/commons/3/30/Holbein-erasmus.jpg.
U.S. Christian Commission: US Library of Congress, Public domain, via Wikimedia Commons, https://upload.wikimedia.org/wikipedia/commons/1/13/Headquarters_of_Christian_Commission%2C_Germantown%2C_Va._34781v.jpg.

Lesson 10
Martin Luther: Lucas Cranach the Elder, Public domain, via Wikimedia Commons, https://upload.wikimedia.org/wikipedia/commons/9/9a/Martin_Luther_by_Cranach-restoration.tif.
Luther 95 Theses: Ferdinand Pauwels, Public domain, via Wikimedia Commons, https://upload.wikimedia.org/wikipedia/commons/2/20/Luther95theses.jpg.

Lesson 11
William Tyndale: See page for author, Public domain, via Wikimedia Commons, https://upload.wikimedia.org/wikipedia/commons/d/d6/Portrait_of_William_Tyndale.jpg.

Lesson 13
Catherine de' Medici: Germain Le Mannier, Public domain, via Wikimedia Commons, https://upload.wikimedia.org/wikipedia/commons/9/9b/Catarina_de%27_Medici_Uffizi.jpg.
Catherine de' Medici: Château de Chenonceau, Public domain, via Wikimedia Commons, https://upload.wikimedia.org/wikipedia/commons/b/b0/Catherine_de_M%C3%A9dicis_Chenonceaux.jpg.
"Hawtins and Kirkpatrick w/Kopp (May 1949)" Newspapers.com. The Los Angeles Times, May 7, 1949. https://www.newspapers.com/article/the-los-angeles-times-hawtins-and-kirkpa/36240592/.

Lesson 13
Queen Mary I: Antonis Mor, Public domain, via Wikimedia Commons, https://upload.wikimedia.org/wikipedia/commons/f/fe/Anthonis_Mor_001.jpg.

Lesson 15
See page for author, CC BY-SA 3.0 <https://creativecommons.org/licenses/by-sa/3.0>, via Wikimedia Commons, https://upload.wikimedia.org/wikipedia/commons/7/7e/Concilio_Trento_Museo_Buonconsiglio.jpg.

Lesson 16
Giorgia Vasari: Circle of Giorgio Vasari, Public domain, via Wikimedia Commons, https://upload.wikimedia.org/wikipedia/commons/d/d2/Vasari%2C_Giorgio-Autoritratto.jpg.

Lesson 17
Shakespeare: Cobbe Collection, Public domain, via Wikimedia Commons, https://upload.wikimedia.org/wikipedia/commons/f/fb/Cobbe_portrait_of_Shakespeare.jpg.

Lesson 18
Galileo: Justus Sustermans, Public domain, via Wikimedia Commons, https://upload.wikimedia.org/wikipedia/commons/d/d4/Justus_Sustermans_-_Portrait_of_Galileo_Galilei%2C_1636.jpg.

Lesson 19
King James: John de Critz, Public domain, via Wikimedia Commons, https://upload.wikimedia.org/wikipedia/commons/b/b0/King_James_I_of_England_and_VI_of_Scotland_by_John_De_Critz_the_Elder.jpg.

Lesson 20
Sir Francis Bacon: National Trust, Public domain, via Wikimedia Commons, https://upload.wikimedia.org/wikipedia/commons/c/ce/British_%28English%29_School_-_Sir_Francis_Bacon_%281561%E2%80%931626%29%2C_1st_Viscount_St_Albans_-_1129151_-_National_Trust.jpg.

IMAGE CREDITS

ID 50184928 © Beatrice Preve | Dreamstime.com (Pisa)
ID 130659726 © Rawpixelimages | Dreamstime.com (landmarks)
ID 82725292 | Gold Frame © Vasilkov | Dreamstime.com (frame)
ID 83600648 | Florence Italy © A1977 | Dreamstime.com (florin)
ID 83326045 | Florence Italy © A1977 | Dreamstime.com (florin)
ID 141198739 | Florence Italy © Zatletic | Dreamstime.com (Saint Mark)
ID 99397538 | Isolated © Sergey Melnikov | Dreamstime.com (astrolabe)
ID 40270810 © Lornet | Dreamstime.com, Leonardo da Vinci's Mona Lisa displayed at the Louvre Museum in Paris, France on August 16, 2009.
ID 217389586 © Giorgio Morara | Dreamstime.com, Leonardo da Vinci's The Last Supper shown on the interior of the refectory of the Convent of Santa Maria delle Grazie in Milan, Italy on June 27, 2018.
ID 133657494 | Leonardo Da Vinci © Dario Rota | Dreamstime.com (Leonardo da Vinci)
ID 8133844 | Antique Frame © Ademdemir | Dreamstime.com (antique frame)
ID 104987610 | Antique © Ruslan Gilmanshin | Dreamstime.com, David from Florence, by Michelangelo
ID 17586707 © Veniamin Kraskov | Dreamstime.com (Michelangelo's David)
ID 31198703 © Cosmin Constantin Sava | Dreamstime.com, Michelangelo's masterpiece: The Creation of Adam in the Sistine Chapel, Vatican Museum on March 08, 2011 in Rome, Italy
ID 22114019 © Gordon Bell | Dreamstime.com (King's College Chapel)
ID 169080883 © Supawat Punnanon | Dreamstime.com (palm tree)
ID 164506800 © Andreykuzmin | Dreamstime.com (brass nameplate)
ID 127157313 © Olga Khorkova | Dreamstime.com (VENICE, ITALY - JUNE 15, 2016 Basilica of Santa Maria Gloriosa dei Frari, The Assumption of the Virgin or Frari Assumption by Titian, close up)
ID 186359920 | William Tyndale © Claudiodivizia | Dreamstime.com (William Tyndale statue)
ID 182790675 © Maurie Hill | Dreamstime.com (Zamosc)
ID 104253971 © Aleksandr Medvedkov | Dreamstime.com (The Louvre)
ID 9799761 © Leelian Chong | Dreamstime.com (antique fork)
ID 21406625 © Gergo Kazsimer | Dreamstime.comm (Celtic Cross)
ID 64399528 © Kabasinki | Dreamstime.com (Library of St. Marks)
ID 6417917 © Chaoss | Dreamstime.com (Grand Canal)
ID 108252862 © Canicula | Dreamstime.com (church)
ID 113493879 © Wisconsinart | Dreamstime.com (vintage van)
ID 7845333 | Harvest © Elena Elisseeva | Dreamstime.com (wheat)
ID 8439800 © Aleksandr Kurganov | Dreamstime.com (bible)
ID 13721166 © Alexey Fursov | Dreamstime.com (nun)
ID 71070214 © David Andrews | Dreamstime.com (William Shakespeare)